"Jessica Harris offers a safe place f... parched souls so they can soak up ... grace. With audacious honesty and raw emotion, Jessica shows how Jesus meets us in the messiness of our lives. He pours healing into our hearts. Pick up this book now. Take a big swig, gulp it down, let it overflow!"

Sam Black, director of recovery education, Covenant Eyes

"Many leaders in the body of Christ have shied away from the fact that in today's culture, pornography addiction is just as much of a women's issue as it is a men's issue. In *Quenched*, Jessica Harris is determined to bring this issue to light within the church. Through testimony, biblical insight, and practical steps, Jessica's book will help women of all ages walk in true freedom."

Ashley Key, cohost, *The 700 Club* and *700 Club Interactive*

"Overcoming a struggle with pornography and shame is not about changing your behavior but about allowing Jesus to transform your identity. Within the pages of this book, you will follow the footsteps of two women who did just that. One is a Samaritan who lived two thousand years ago, and the other is Jessica Harris, a friend who courageously unveils that you can find freedom. Journey with them, and you will find genuine hope as they lead you to the living water."

Dr. Juli Slattery, president/cofounder of Authentic Intimacy, author of *Rethinking Sexuality* and *Sex and the Single Girl*

"Jessica Harris is a trailblazer and a fighter for girls and women seeking to overcome pornography and sexual shame. Her new book, *Quenched*, helps you to see God and yourself through the lens of grace rather than shame. As overcomers of decades-long pornography addictions, we cannot recommend this book enough."

The Victory Collective

"I met Jessica Harris years ago when we both were in the earlier season of our ministries to women bound up in sexual shame. Reading *Quenched* was an encouraging, Christ-exalting way to get to know her all over again and to be inspired afresh that Jesus is the life, love, freedom, and healing that all of us desire and need. This book will draw you to Jesus, give hope for your journey of faith, and offer courage to be set free from pornography's grip."

Ellen Mary Dykas, author of *Toxic Relationships*

Quenched

Quenched

Discovering God's
Abundant Grace
for Women
Struggling with
Pornography and
Sexual Shame

JESSICA HARRIS

BakerBooks
a division of Baker Publishing Group
Grand Rapids, Michigan

© 2023 by Jessica Harris

Published by Baker Books
a division of Baker Publishing Group
PO Box 6287, Grand Rapids, MI 49516-6287
www.bakerbooks.com

Printed in the United States of America

Library of Congress Cataloging-in-Publication Data
Names: Harris, Jessica, 1985– author.
Title: Quenched : discovering God's abundant grace for women struggling with pornography and sexual shame / Jessica Harris.
Description: Grand Rapids, MI : Baker Books, a division of Baker Publishing Group, [2023] | Includes bibliographical references.
Identifiers: LCCN 2022020836 | ISBN 9781540902269 (paperback) | ISBN 9781540903037 (casebound) | ISBN 9781493439577 (ebook)
Subjects: LCSH: Christian women—Religious life. | Shame—Religious aspects—Christianity. | Pornography—Religious aspects—Christianity | Sex—Religious aspects—Christianity. | God (Christianity)—Love.
Classification: LCC BV4527 .H38548 2023 | DDC 248.8/43—dc23/eng/20220708
LC record available at https://lccn.loc.gov/2022020836

Some names and details have been changed to protect the privacy of the individuals involved.

The described traumatic events in the author's life are her recollections/opinions of the events that occurred and may not match the memories of those involved.

All italics in Scripture quotations are the author's emphasis.

Published in association with Books & Such Literary Management, www.books andsuch.com.

Baker Publishing Group publications use paper produced from sustainable forestry practices and post-consumer waste whenever possible.

23 24 25 26 27 28 29   7 6 5 4 3 2 1

To my daughters, Naomi and Marie.
My highest calling in life
is showing you the unfailing, unending,
unconditional love of God.

I pray that you, being rooted and firmly established in love, may be able to comprehend with all the saints what is the length and width, height and depth of God's love, and to know Christ's love that surpasses knowledge, so that you may be filled with all the fullness of God.

EPHESIANS 3:17–19 CSB

Contents

Foreword by Phylicia
Masonheimer   11

Introduction   13

1. Cries from the Well   23

2. The Long Walk to the Well   34

3. The Desire to Be Known   48

4. The Desire to Be Free   62

5. The Desire to Be Loved   78

6. The Desire to Worship   92

7. The Desire for Healing   109

8. A Long Walk Redeemed   124

9. A Desire Satisfied   138

10. Living Life Quenched   152

Conclusion: *Now What?* 165

Appendix A: *A Special Letter to Those Who Don't Struggle* 183

Appendix B: *Setting Up a Recovery Community* 189

Acknowledgments 195

Notes 199

About the Author 203

Foreword

I was exposed to erotica—pornographic novels—at a garage sale when I was twelve.

I grew up in a healthy Christian home. I was homeschooled. I had engaged, Christian parents who loved each other and their kids. My story of addiction and sexual shame didn't fit the narrative around women and pornography. At least, that's how it felt. It wasn't supposed to happen to me.

Why me? I asked that question for many years. I also wondered, *Why did I find that book? Why have I had to struggle with pornography for more than a decade? Why doesn't God DO something?*

Over the next few years I found answers to those questions. I learned just how kind, how good, and how loving God is toward me, and that grace freed me from my addiction, empowering me to share that freedom with other women still trapped in shame.

But if I could change one thing, have it all over, I dearly wish I'd had a resource like *Quenched*. When I was struggling with erotic novels, there were few, if any, resources for women wrestling with pornography. It was a "man's sport." The church was eerily silent on the topic, and speaking up about addiction took great courage (and still does!). If *Quenched* had existed when I was an ashamed teenager living a double life, would I have found freedom sooner?

We will never know what my story would have been had Jessica's work existed years ago, but I am grateful God redeemed me from that path in spite of my lack of resources. I am immensely *more* grateful that women today have access to this book. The message in these pages is a clarion call of hope. Hope for the girl who thinks she's too far gone. Hope for the girl who thinks purity isn't possible. Hope for the girl who thinks she's in too deep to dig her way out.

Perhaps we wrestle with hopelessness in part because we know there's a kernel of truth in it. We *can't* dig our way out of pornography and addiction. If you've ever tried to check off the days when you haven't clicked the link, read the book, or sinned in secret, you know exactly what I'm talking about. Willpower can't redeem us. No one is strong enough to climb out of a pit so deep. That's why the gospel is so beautiful. While we are still in the pit, Jesus reaches down inside of it and pulls us out.

I was in the pit, and he pulled me out. If he can do it for me and for Jessica, he can do it for you too.

As you read this book, I pray the goodness of the gospel becomes real for you. Jesus meant these words when he said them; we get to trust that they are true: "So if the Son sets you free, you will be free indeed" (John 8:36).

Phylicia Masonheimer
Founder and CEO, Every Woman a Theologian

Introduction

By way of introductions, let's just start here: my name is Jessica Harris and I used to be addicted to pornography. Yes, I am a woman who struggled with pornography.

When I share my story, people tend to react in one of three ways: shock, disbelief, or hope. Some are shocked a woman could have this struggle. They immediately question what must be wrong with my wiring. I watch their view of me change right before my eyes. What kind of woman must I be?

"Why?" a pastor asked me after a speaking event. "I mean, I understand why men do this, but women? *Why*?"

Others struggle to believe what I am saying is true. They cannot believe women struggle with lust or porn use at all. Their most common response is to ask for clarity or qualify what I must actually mean. They assume that by "pornography" I mean erotica, and by "struggle" I mean "I read it a couple of times a year." Surely I must be exaggerating.

But there is a group who understands exactly what I mean. When I say pornography, they know I mean pornography—not romance novels or "mommy" porn. They know I mean the kind of porn "the men" struggle with. They know what I mean when I say addicted. They know it's more than just a couple of times a year or once a week. They know the struggle of being a woman who feels trapped by hardcore pornography, lust, fantasy, masturbation—any combination or all of the above. And they know the crippling shame that comes with it.

If you fall into that category, this book is for you.

How This Book Began

One summer afternoon while I was visiting my grandparents' home, the one where I spent seven years of my childhood, I made my way to the room that used to be mine. I climbed onto my old bed, now covered in cat hair and smelling of woodsmoke. I stared at the ceiling and allowed my heart to wander down old, broken trails.

It's fitting this story began there, because *my* story of sexual struggle and shame began there too. I experienced some of the most devastating pain a young child could ever endure there. As a first grader, I returned to this home to find my father had packed his bags and left us. For years, I cried in this room, sprawled across this same bed, writing letters begging my father to come home. I hid in this room from the brokenness that, at times, crippled my family with anger and rage.

A couple of years after my father left, an elementary school classmate molested me on the school bus. That encounter filled me with so much confusion and shame. At school, he forced me to kiss him. A classmate told a teacher, and despite my attempts to explain what happened, we both got in trouble. I tried to explain to my teachers and my family that

I wasn't comfortable with him, but I lacked the vocabulary to explain why. They told me I needed to be nice.

For years after, he would come to my grandparents' home bearing gifts for me. I would escape to my room, and he would follow so we could "talk." He'd sit beside me on my bed and my skin would crawl. I'd sit as close as I could to the head of the bed, staring into the closet, longing for him to leave.

My mother, siblings, and I moved away from it all when I was thirteen, but every time I came back to visit my grandparents, I encountered a mix of comfort and brokenness, joy and immense pain.

We all learn many lessons in our homes. I learned to snap fresh green beans with Gramma out on the back porch swing. She taught me how to play piano by setting me on her lap and pressing my fingers to the keys. Grampa taught me how to take care of a garden and pick the ripest strawberries—one for the basket, one for me.

My grandparents also taught me about Jesus. Many Sunday mornings I would wake to the sound of aerosol glue as Gramma made her flannelgraphs for Sunday school. At meals, Grampa would pray for our food. When he prayed, I felt like I had just been ushered into a sacred place. Every night, as I went to bed, I would see him sitting at the edge of his bed reading the Bible while sipping his final cup of coffee for the day. The light would shine through the doorway of my bedroom, accompanied by the clinking of the spoon against his porcelain mug. Yet, amid all the life lessons and bittersweet memories, the lessons that affected my heart the most were the ones I learned about shame.

Lying on my old mattress as a grown woman brought back to memory the days I had lain there staring at the ceiling, crying, desperate for healing, for acceptance, for someone to truly love little broken me and chase after my heart.

How Shame Began

In a way, this home is where I learned to be ashamed of my brokenness. Where I learned to shut up and stop crying. Where I had to be nice to the boy who had taken a piece of my innocence. Where I learned my struggle with pornography was sick, twisted, and unacceptable. In this home, I learned about Jesus and also learned he probably found me disgusting. I learned God was love, but I was unworthy of that love because of what I had done.

Shame isn't something we necessarily set out to teach. As a mom now, I realize shame is often a byproduct of frustration and feelings of inconvenience. It's the message that who we are is unacceptable. It's the message that love is dependent on performance, obedience, and meeting a certain standard. When we fail to meet a standard, shame tells us we have to fight for, prove, and earn our worth.

But shame wasn't a message limited to the four walls of my grandparents' home. It was one I heard in church as well. My grandparents had attended the same church for decades. The church that turned its back on my family when my dad left. The church with the Christian school where I first learned about sex through the crude jokes of my elementary school classmates, including the boy on the school bus. The church where I spent my teen years trying to convince the world I had my life together, hiding my addiction to hardcore pornography.

I was exposed to pornography by accident when I was thirteen years old. My family had just moved from my grandparents' home to our own place. One day, as I researched for a school project, I found a website full of educational video clips. Nestled among these clips was a video with an odd title and a dark, blurry thumbnail. Curious, I clicked. In a matter of seconds, I was exposed to hardcore pornography.

As I tried to close the window, I encountered pop-up after pop-up, crippling my ability to escape. Those pop-up windows led me to a site filled with violent hardcore pornography. Multiple videos filled the screen, new ones loading every few seconds. I was a mix of traumatized, confused, and mesmerized. For me, this answered some of the questions that had been in my mind for years.

So, this is why the boy on the bus did that to me.

Oh, so this is what my classmates were talking about.

But for every answered question, there was another new question. And so began my journey into hardcore pornography. It quickly consumed my life. What started as innocent exposure and curiosity morphed into deliberate, deceitful obsession. Within four years, I was watching porn for hours a day, masturbating several times a day, reading erotica on school computers, and staying up late at night tuned in to the adult channels we did not get in hopes that a scene would slip through.

Where Grace Began

I had quite a journey to freedom, a journey marked by a constant battle with shame. And after I finally found freedom, I began sharing my story. But that day, on that old bed, I realized it had been a while since I had really given thought to how God's grace intersected with that story. I don't know what was so special about that particular visit to my grand-parents' house—the visit where this book first began to take shape. Perhaps it was the sermon that morning, which led my heart to reflect on the story of the woman at the well. Whatever it was, that day in that room, as I thought of John 4, I had a fresh encounter with grace.

I had heard this passage countless times in church, but taking time to think about it revealed so many parallels to my own story. It revealed the toxic, isolating, hope-sucking nature of shame and forced it to stand in stark contrast with grace. The Jesus of John 4 stood in direct opposition to the Jesus I'd been taught about in this house and in the halls of that church.

That day, I faced one of the most impactful decisions of my life. I had a choice to make: to keep holding on to what I had been taught about God or to believe what he said about himself. I had to choose between shame and grace.

For hours while I lay on that bed, I read the story, studied the text, wrote, and encountered God's grace anew in my life. I hoped, even then, to one day write a book both confronting the destructive shame that held me captive and sharing God's heart.

In the meantime, I shared my story in churches around the world in a new presentation called "The Long Walk to the Well." The title speaks to the shame so many women face as they struggle with lust and sexual sin and highlights the gentle grace and heart of God that longs to see them set free.

The Price of Shame

We are created for intimacy, not isolation. We are designed for relationship—relationship with each other, relationship with God. Shame stands in direct opposition to that message. Shame tells you every connection you have is fragile, and if you were truly and fully known, you would be alone. It delivers the clear message that you are a hypocrite, will never be free, and will never be worthy of connection. While your heart may long to lose the mask, shame will force you to hold it tighter.

In some cases, shame becomes a self-fulfilling prophecy. It's the worship leader who stands at the front on a Sunday morning all the while thinking, *If they really knew who I am . . .* It's the wife who is too afraid to tell her husband about her struggle for fear she will lose his love. It's the daughter who feels her family will disown her if they find out.

In my life, no relationship suffered the devastating effects of shame more than my relationship with God. In the depths of my struggle, I believed he found me disgusting. I imagined him as a disappointed father, frustrated with each failure.

Even as I walked in freedom and victory from pornography and began to share my story and see other people find freedom, I couldn't shake the feeling of being an exile. It felt like the scarlet letter of pornography was seared deep into my soul. No matter how hard I tried to erase it, the label would always be there. Faded, perhaps, but I assumed it would never leave. Maybe, someday, I would be able to approach God without this hanging over me, but I struggled to shake the feeling of being unworthy, gross, and unlovable.

That all changed the day I reflected on the story of Jesus and the woman at the well. I came to understand God's heart for me in ways I never had before. This revelation gave me a renewed sense of freedom and life.

God wasn't disgusted with me. He didn't view me as a dirty, rotten, no-good sinner. He loved me. I wasn't a hostile stranger but instead a beloved daughter. My struggle didn't surprise him and, unlike the Christian "experts" who surrounded me, he knew I wasn't the first woman in the world to have this particular struggle.

My heart in writing this book is to take you on that same journey. We've all heard "Jesus loves me." We've sung it, repeated it, and said we believed it. If you're honest, though, there is likely a part of you, deep down, where the faintest whisper tells you it isn't true for you. Jesus loves *everyone else*. But you? You managed to screw up so badly. You managed to fall so far. You managed to do something so hideous God's love and grace cannot reach you where you are. But, my friend, such a place does not exist.

The Journey Ahead

We're going to walk through the journey of the woman in John 4. We don't know much about her, so please allow me some creative license to make connections from her story to ours. The point isn't the factual details of her story as much as it is seeing God's heart for her. It's the same heart he has for us.

If a struggle with pornography isn't part of your story, and you've picked this book up to help someone else, thank you. We need more people like you who are willing to start the hard conversations. I have a special letter for you in appendix A, and I invite you to read that first.

These pages are divided into several sections. First, we'll discuss the setting of this story and why it matters. Then, we'll talk about the different desires of our hearts, how those desires manifest in our struggles, and how God longs to meet them. Finally, we'll wrap up with a bit of practical application.

Do me a favor: don't skip to the practical application part. I know it is tempting. One of my quirks is wanting to watch the end of the movie before I see the beginning. This is how I watched the entire *Lord of the Rings* trilogy—essentially in reverse. I would happen upon my family watching it, sit down with them, and, much to my brothers' dismay, pelt them with questions. "Who is that elf?" "What's the deal with the big fiery eyeball?" (Yes, I am that person who talks during a movie.) Call it anxiety; call it impatience. I call it efficiency. If the ending is good, then I assume the beginning will be worth my time. The next time the movie would play, I would watch a little more of it.

But some things in life cannot be done backward. If you have struggled with pornography or lust for any amount of time, you've likely tried to break free on your own. You, like all of us, want the easy formula, the 1-2-3. You might have picked up this book hoping for a breakdown of all the practical steps you need to take to end this struggle once and for all. You're frustrated with your failures and empty promises to "never do it again."

I understand the pain of this struggle, the crushing weight of shame, and the desperation to just be free. But as someone who has been there, let me tell you, there are no practical steps that can set us free. No formula, no program, no book, even. Only Jesus can free us.

But so many of us believe Jesus expects us to free ourselves first. We think he wants us to pick the lock on our prison cell and arrange our own escape. We imagine him waiting at some far-off rendezvous point while we embark on an epic journey, like the hobbits of Middle-earth desperate to throw the ring of our iniquity and struggle into the fires of Mordor. We tell ourselves, *Once I get this under control,* then *I'll read my Bible,* then *I'll pray, and* then *God will love me.*

We have it all wrong. Our formula is backward. We don't get ourselves free first and then experience God's love. We experience God's love first and then we know freedom.

So, please do not skip to the end thinking I'm going to give you ten practical steps for ending your struggle, because ending the struggle isn't the most important thing right now. Contrary to what your church or family or others may have led you to believe, God loves us even when we are struggling. That is where we have to start. That is the connection we have to make.

If we don't believe God's love intends to meet us in our struggle, we will remain trapped. We may find freedom from pornography or lust, but we will continue to be hemmed in by shame. We will remain caged in performance, anxiety, and the belief that his love is for everyone but us. We will believe his love comes with a price.

That isn't the gospel. That isn't the message of God's love. And if you want to experience freedom, *true* freedom, it doesn't start with password protecting your computer, smashing your iPhone, or burning your stash of romance novels. It doesn't start with confronting your sin head-on and trying to beat it. The journey starts where so many of us think it ends, in the place so many of us fear the most: an encounter with Jesus.

CHAPTER 1

Cries from the Well

Do you believe God desires you?

It's probably easy to believe God loves you. Doesn't he love everybody? And, of course, you know God knows you. After all, he knows everything.

You may even believe he wants you. But "want" is less like passion and more like those "Uncle Sam wants you" posters with a patriotic old man jabbing his finger in your face to recruit you to join an army. It brings to mind the children's Sunday school song "I'm in the Lord's Army." We like to think God finds us useful.

But *desire*? That feels scandalous.

As women who struggle with pornography or lust, we know a thing or two about desire. That deep longing. That craving. That need—not because we actually need it but because we really want it. In a sense, desire feels a lot like lust—the thing that got us into this mess in the first place.

Wasn't it desire that drew you to shut the door behind you and fire up the screen? Isn't it desire's voice you hear calling in the waking hours of the morning, demanding to be satisfied? It seems desire leads us into secret places to do secret things we later secretly regret.

So the idea of God desiring me causes me to pause and ask, "Come again?"

I know me, and after knowing me for a long time, my first impulse is to say there is nothing in me worth desiring. God must have the wrong girl. He's got his wires crossed.

Now, if he needs something, sign me up. Need me to do something? Need a performance? Need a problem solved? Need something to be managed? I'm there. I'm loyal to a fault, people say. I'd be a missionary to a far-off country if he asked. But there is no way God could desire me *for me*. He has to desire something *from* me. If not usefulness, then at least obedience. Not just a nontransactional relationship.

I struggled with the same idea when I met and married my husband. It made no sense to me why he—why any man, really—would want me. I feel like most days I'm a calloused INTJ critic with frizzy hair, chunky thighs, too many freckles, and not enough positivity. Even though I don't demand thousand-dollar handbags or require hours to get ready for the day, I still feel high maintenance. My husband would call me my own worst critic.

Of course I am. I *know* me. I know my trauma and my insecurities. My past addiction and my haunting memories. I know the depths and darkness of my own heart. I've hung out with myself for a while, and if I ran into me at a party, I wouldn't want to hang out with me.

In the middle of our struggle, or even after we've found freedom, we can feel far from desirable and remarkably alone.

Let's Talk Statistics

We put a lot of faith and energy into statistics. Leaders will use surveys, studies, and percentages to determine focal points and make strategies to tackle big issues. We choose our priorities based on how prevalent a need seems to be. When the church views statistics that say over 60 percent of men and 1 in 7 pastors struggle with pornography, it makes sense to address these struggles at men's conferences and pancake breakfasts.[1] The church has been relatively silent about women and their struggle with pornography simply because the statistics don't seem to merit a reaction.

Even though I taught high school math for five years, I have a problem with statistics. We simply don't know how to apply them correctly. It is human nature to believe that the worst will never happen to us and the best will, regardless of the statistics. The lottery is a great example. The odds of winning the lottery are staggering. We're talking only 1 in over 300 million.[2] Still, people play. We can be irrational idealists at times. We believe the odds for good things are better than they are, and the odds for unpleasant things are worse. Fact: it is more likely we will die in a car crash than win the lottery, but we still drive our cars to the gas station to buy our tickets.[3]

So, no, we don't know how to use statistics correctly. We use them to our advantage when they are in our favor. When they are not, we ignore them.

In a room full of pastors, it's hard to look around at others and think, *Someone in my circle struggles with pornography.* It's easier to tell ourselves, *No, not that person! Surely it's the pastor of the church down the street, not my fishing buddy.*

I know what it's like to stand face-to-face with data that says my story doesn't exist. I found myself addicted to pornography, and at age seventeen I was desperate for a way out. Pornography had consumed my life. But when I looked for help, I found none and felt alone. I convinced myself I must be the only woman in the world who had managed to get herself into this mess.

When I went off to college, I actually hoped to get caught. It made sense that my conservative small-town church might not know what to do, but I assumed the staff at a Christian college would. I did get caught in college, but instead of finding help, I ran into even more shame. The dean of women told me, "We know this wasn't you. Women just don't have this problem." But she was wrong. In the years since, I've realized just how wrong.

When I struggled with pornography, I believed that out of the entire female population on the planet, I was the only one who had managed to get stuck with that addiction. There just weren't statistics for women at the time. Now there are. A recent study published in the *Journal of Sex Research* indicated that up to 60 percent of women were consuming some form of pornography (video, picture, or written) at least monthly.[4] And in case you're thinking that's all the women "out there" but not Christian women, a 2016 study by Barna showed almost 20 percent of Christian women use porn regularly. In the study's notes, Barna indicates that underreporting is possible because "porn use within the Christian community is much less socially acceptable than in the wider culture."[5] In other words, the *real* numbers are likely higher.

You Are Not Alone

And still, here you are, believing you are all alone. You struggle, some faceless other Christian women struggle, but there is no way anyone you know struggles. There is no way your best friend is into porn—or your pastor's daughter, or your pastor's wife, or your pastor herself. You, despite the statistics and studies, believe you are alone. This is one of the hallmarks of shame.

The following excerpts are stories sent to me over the past ten years by readers of my blog. They represent many similar stories from wives, ministry leaders, daughters, sisters, and friends affected by a struggle with lust. Each is shared with permission, but names are changed and personally identifying information has been removed.

If you are a woman who struggles, I hope you will know you are not alone. If this isn't your struggle, I hope you will see how deeply the owners of these stories ache to feel the quenching power of grace. The statistics say someone in your life is struggling, and they might be feeling the same things these women express. You have a chance to step in and help change their story.

Esther

Esther was exposed to porn when she was nine years old. She would tell you her twelve-year-long struggle started all because of curiosity. She was caught several times but continued to delve further and further into pornography, fully engulfed in it by the time she was thirteen.

It pulled me further from God in a time when I needed him most. It brought on a lot of anxiety, fear, and depression. None of which I had before. It started running my decisions. Instead of running an errand or studying for school, I would intentionally just lock myself into watching porn and/or masturbating. I lost a lot of friendships because I couldn't stop thinking about my own problems and talking about them. It put my helping into overdrive. I've always been a helpful person but I started to almost try to fix others because I couldn't fix my own life.

Jamie

I remember the day I stumbled upon [pornography]. Around age nine, I was home. We had our TV set up, and it was our first week of having cable. I was so ecstatic that I faked being sick to stay home from school and watch TV. I saw an image of a nearly naked woman. I cannot remember what I searched for or how I got to it, but next thing you know, I was finding ways to access porn right on my family's desktop computer.

As the years went on, I found ways to be sneaky about my struggle. I cannot remember the extent of the struggle, as far as how often I would view it, but I remember being confused as a little girl trying to understand if what I was doing was sinful. All I knew is that I did not want anyone to know.

Up until I was fourteen years old, I was keeping this secret pretty well. But I guess I did not cover my tracks well enough, because my parents found my search history. They loved me enough to sit me down and talk with me about it. But of course, with my "good girl" approach to life and my desire to keep this a secret, I just remember the shame I felt. They were so gracious and loving to me, but that didn't rid me of my shame. . . .

I may have stopped viewing for a little bit of time after my parents talked to me, but it was an on-again-off-again struggle throughout high school. My freshman year of college was a mess in regard to my pornography use. I was making friends fine in college, but I was really struggling with the transition from home to this new area I was in and grieving the loss of what life was like before with my family and friends at home. . . .

What I mostly remember is my struggle with pornography and masturbation becoming more of an addiction than ever before. It was an every night ordeal. And I felt a chasm growing in my relationship with God at a rapidly high speed. I was watching porn every night and then crying myself to sleep. Some nights I felt hysterical because I wanted this sin to be taken from me, but I felt so powerless. I perceived God was angry with me. He did not want anything to do with me. Why would he? I was dirty and couldn't fix it.

Charlotte

Tell me, what do you do when you feel so helpless? What do you do when you feel like no one cares enough to understand and to help? When God feels distant . . . is God even there? Tell me, what do you do when there is no hope? I am twenty-one years old, and I have struggled with pornography since I was eleven.

I was invited to a slumber party by my best friend where she had us watch pornographic movies. Those images have never left my mind. It became a whirlwind of internet searches and masturbation. Regret and guilt. Waking up and feeling disgusted, wanting to die, hating myself, and never knowing how to get out. . . .

I cried to God for years, begging him to take this away from me. I feel he never did, and I am trapped. This caused me to lose all hope in God. I know there is a God, but he's not on my side.

I don't know what to do anymore. I have lost hope in all healing. I don't have the patience to go on. I feel so broken. . . .

Satan, as you can well imagine, uses this to remind me how because of this, I will never be able to truly love a man without bringing filth into it. And quite frankly, it just breaks my heart. Because this does seem to be the case. I do not want to look at the man that I love and take an immediate trail to my sexual dysfunction.

I'm asking you to just please pray. I don't think anyone can fix this but God, and I am at the end of my rope begging him to relieve me of this.

I have received hundreds of stories like these. The statistics won't tell you any of them. The statistics won't tell you about the church youth leader who called me because an anonymous survey showed 100 percent of the group's ninth and tenth grade girls struggled with pornography.

The statistics won't tell you the story of the Christian high school student who came forward at an event after I shared my own story of porn addiction and sexting. She had written her story on a slip of paper and handed it to me with tears streaming down her face. After reading her story, I flipped the paper over to read, in all caps, "I FEEL SO LOST."

Statistics won't tell you the sobs that racked her body as I prayed with her to know God's grace and forgiveness. Statistics don't tell the stories of redemption.

Your Story Matters

In my years of speaking out on this topic, I have seen people try to overanalyze this struggle among women. They assume (wrongly) that if a woman struggles with pornography, then she must have a history of sexual abuse. Or she must have a father wound. They want to know the algorithms and the metrics. "What kind of woman struggles with pornography?" they ask.

There isn't a "story template" for this. Women who struggle come from any and every background. Your family may be broken and marked by abuse and abandonment, or it may be picture-perfect and full of love, camaraderie, and belonging. You may have grown up in church or come to Jesus as an adult. You may have been sexually abused or grown up with healthy examples of sexuality around you.

I don't know your story, but I do know God's story, and I invite you into it. I also know this: no matter where you are, who you are, what you've done, or what has been done to you, God desires you.

Shame's most powerful work is convincing us that we are undesirable and alone. If you believe you are the only person who has landed where you are and that God wants nothing to do with you because of it, shame has the upper hand. It has cut you off and exiled you from all hope of connection, healing, and grace. If you believe you are alone, shame is at work. But shame is also wrong. Finally, we are seeing the statistics that prove we are not alone, but even if there were no statistics, we'd be left with a lifeline: grace.

Grace doesn't depend on statistics.

There are only three statistics God cares about: all, none, and everyone.

For *all* have sinned and fall short of the glory of God. (Rom. 3:23)

None is righteous, no, not one. (v. 10 ESV)

Everyone who calls on the name of the Lord will be saved. (10:13)

That is the message of the gospel and grace. In a culture overwhelmed by statistics, that is the truth that sets us free. It doesn't matter if we are one in a million, one in one hundred, or one in ten. God is a Shepherd who leaves the ninety-nine sheep in pursuit of the one. The one isn't disposable or insignificant. Priority isn't given to the ninety-nine simply because they outnumber the one. No, he pursues the one.

While we tend to devote all our resources to the demands of the largest percentage, God seemingly operates in reverse. Instead of directing all his efforts to the ninety-nine who are safe, he gives everything he has for the one who needs his help. Grace ignores the statistics dictating our resources and pursues stories to change them. That is, after all, the purpose of grace: it redeems and changes our stories.

So while a pastor, parent, or leader may look at statistics and think, *That's not that big of a deal,* God knows the truth. And the truth is, to the one, it is a very big deal. Your one story is significant to him. You are significant to him. He desires you.

CHAPTER 2

The Long Walk
to the Well

Shame isn't a new enemy. Trace our story back to Genesis, and shame enters the picture rather quickly, making a mess of the "very good" and severing the sweetest of relationships. Adam and Eve enjoyed walks with God in the garden of Eden, unhindered fellowship with the Creator of the universe, and unbridled intimacy with each other. The end of Genesis 2 tells us they were both naked and not ashamed. But soon everything changed.

As we read through the creation story in Genesis, we see Eve tricked, deceived by a serpent who casts doubt on God's goodness and calls into question God's intentions. Eve listens, and the world is never the same. After her and Adam's forbidden feast, God comes looking for them in the garden, and they hide. Adam gives his reasoning: "I was afraid because I was naked; so I hid" (Gen. 3:10). This is humanity's first encounter with shame.

Adam had always been naked, and it hadn't been a problem before. The problem came when he realized his nakedness and thought he needed to hide it. He doubted. He disobeyed, and because he did, God became a threat, someone Adam needed to hide from. The intimacy and relationship between husband and wife and between Creator and creation changed dramatically, marked and marred by shame.

We follow the same pattern in our lives when it comes to struggles with sin, especially sin of a sexual nature. God has a plan for this desire he's given us, this desire to be connected intimately with another person, this tree planted in the middle of our lives. But there's always an enemy—an enemy of God, an enemy of us, an enemy of intimacy—who loves to slither in and cast doubt on God's goodness and call into question his intention. Shame lies waiting just beyond our doubt and our decision to disobey.

Years ago, as I searched the radio for something to listen to during my drive to a speaking engagement, I came across a talk show on abstinence, of all things. The show featured two Christians debating about saving sex for marriage. One woman said, "What if I never get married? I can't believe a good God would expect me to die without experiencing sexual pleasure."

At the bottom of all of our struggles is this same spirit of question and confusion: "Is this *really* what God said?" "Is that *really* what he meant?" "But what about . . . ?"

All of this questioning leads us to be tempted by things that will never satisfy. It leads us to pornography, lust, fantasy, masturbation, even sexting and hooking up. And then, like Adam and Eve, we quickly find ourselves thrown into shame.

Sex, by its very nature, is intimate, vulnerable, and personal. When we struggle with sexual sins or unwanted sexual behaviors, there is an added level of shame, a feeling of exposure, of nakedness, and, for some, of deep-down dirtiness.

I once heard *character* defined as who you are when no one is watching and the doors are all closed. We hear something like that, look at our lives of secret sins, and know we're naked. So we hide. We hide from God and others. We cut off relationships. We build walls. We sew fig leaves together and frantically try to cover up who we are.

Brené Brown is a well-known "shame researcher." In discussing the difference between guilt and shame, she has this to say:

> I define shame as the intensely painful feeling or experience of believing that we are flawed and therefore unworthy of love and belonging—something we've experienced, done, or failed to do makes us unworthy of connection.
>
> I don't believe shame is helpful or productive. I think shame is much more likely to be the source of destructive, hurtful behavior than the solution or cure. I think the fear of disconnection can make us dangerous.[1]

A Look at John

In John 4, we meet a woman who, according to some Bible teachers, is in this place of shame and disconnection. At first glance, it seems like just another story in this Gospel's collection. John, more than the other Gospels, reads like a compilation of Jesus's personal interactions with people. The beginning of the book outlines Christ's call to many of the disciples. In chapter 3, we see Jesus's encounter with Nicodemus. In chapter 4, we meet the woman at the well. Later in the book are stories of healings and the resurrection of Lazarus. After Christ's death and resurrection, John details Jesus's encounter with Mary Magdalene and, finally, his reconciliation with Simon Peter.

The book is summed up with this moving statement:

> Jesus performed many other signs in the presence of his disciples, which are not recorded in this book. But these are written that you may believe that Jesus is the Messiah, the Son of God, and that by believing you may have life in his name. (20:30–31)

Some of these interactions, like the encounter we're going to explore, were private encounters between Jesus and another person. Jesus must have shared these stories with the disciples. If he hadn't, then John 4 would simply read, "We traveled into Samaria, left Jesus at a well, and went into town to get food. When we came back, we found him talking to some woman. She left and then came back with the whole town. The end."

Instead, we are offered a narrative of what happened at that well. And I believe the reason this story and many others in John were captured is to show us the very personal nature of our Savior.

Why highlight private, one-on-one interactions with people if not to show us how God longs to interact with us individually? The Jesus who fed the five thousand is the same Jesus who wept with Mary and Martha over the loss of their brother, Lazarus (John 11). The Jesus who looked on the masses and had compassion (Mark 6) is the same Jesus who defended a woman caught in adultery (John 8).

When we are weighed down under shame, it's all too easy to view ourselves as insignificant. We feel lost and unimportant. We feel unworthy of God's time, love, interaction, and grace. But the message of grace breaks through our shame and gives our lives value, purpose, and identity.

As we look at John 4, I feel it is important to point out that there are some varying opinions about what type of story this is. Some allege that this encounter is symbolic, and that the five husbands Jesus mentions stand for the five tribes of Israel represented in her town.[2] Others suggest the five husbands refer to the five pagan gods of Samaria, and that this encounter serves as a rebuke to Samaria for their idolatry.[3]

To be sure, this encounter is filled with symbolism, and we will certainly explore some of that as we dive into the passage. For a baseline, though, I want to approach this passage as most scholars and Bible teachers do: this was a literal woman from Samaria, who had literally been with five men before the one she was currently with. This literal woman had a literal encounter with a literal Jesus at a literal well, and it literally changed her town. The pages ahead will contain some assumptions because the text doesn't make everything clear, but I will try to point those out as I can.

We are going to focus on God's heart for us, using her story as a sort of road map. We're going to concentrate less on her backstory and more on Jesus's response to her, the desires she expressed in the narrative, and how Jesus wanted to meet those desires.

The Setting for Shame

This story took place at a well, in Samaria, at high noon. The disciples went into town, leaving a weary Jesus behind to rest. Then a woman came to draw water.

If you've grown up in church, perhaps you've heard more than one sermon on this passage and its unusual setup. Jesus shouldn't have been in Samaria. Why didn't he stay with his disciples? And what on earth was this woman doing drawing water from the well at noon, which was not a typical time of day to get water?

This woman's act of drawing water from a well wasn't like popping by the drinking fountain to fill up your water bottle. Water was needed for many things: cooking, cleaning, bathing, drinking. A twenty-ounce bottle wasn't going to be enough for her. She'd need gallons of water every day to be able to function, and water is heavy.

If you needed to walk down to the corner store and haul home a five-gallon jug of water (weighing over forty pounds), you likely wouldn't choose to go at noon. If you *did* go at noon, that choice likely would be motivated by necessity. Now, that necessity could very well be that you ran out of water for cooking and needed to refill sooner rather than later. However, that necessity could also be that you just wanted to be alone—or that you feel you *deserved* to be alone.

I asked some of my readers to describe shame, and here's what they said:

Shame causes me to isolate myself.
Shame makes me feel unworthy of being treated like a human and makes me pull away from relationships.

Shame causes me to hide. I feel like people only love me for my "masked self."

I distance myself from people I respect. I go into hiding.

Shame, by its nature, isolates. It severs relationships and causes us to withdraw.

What if, as many Bible teachers have surmised, shame motivated this woman's choice to draw water at noon, all alone?[4] What if her decision served as a way to make sure she saw no one and would avoid the judging eyes, the condescending stares? What if this was the "easier" choice?

That would mean every day, every step the Samaritan woman took would remind her of her choices, her worth, her value. In a way, her walk to the well served as punishment. She felt she deserved every step in the hot sun. She had only herself to blame for every bead of sweat, every aching muscle. A normal task of everyday life had become a form of torture, of penance.

Isn't this how shame operates in our own lives? When we live under the mantle of shame, the most benign daily tasks can become torturous. We each have some version of a "long walk to the well," something that shame has affected deeply. Shame makes us skip girls' night out. It makes us turn down a coffee date with a friend. It makes us sit by ourselves at lunch.

We see our desires for connection and relationship as dangerous and ourselves as defective. Maybe you've seen this play out in your own life. What many would see as the simplest of tasks or relationships has become a burden for you.

A young wife who shared her story with me told me she had struggled with pornography throughout high school, but she found freedom in college, where she also met her future husband. During their engagement, she shared her past struggle with him and told him she had been walking in freedom. However, she had an affair while her fiancé was studying abroad and chose to hide it from him. When he returned, she ended the affair but dove headfirst back into pornography.

Afraid he would leave her, she kept her secret. She kept assuring herself that once they were married, she would feel comfortable enough to be honest and share. Instead, their marriage drove her to fear even more. The fear of telling him and the shame for her choices completely overwhelmed her to the point she couldn't experience an intimate relationship with her husband. To overcome the mental and emotional block of shame, she would have to excuse herself to the bathroom, where she would watch porn on her phone to get in the mood.

Imagine being so overwhelmed by shame that even the most intimate of relationships is a trigger. For this woman, her long walk to the well became the walk to her bedroom every night. Every kiss from her husband drove a dagger deeper into her heart.

The Symptoms of Shame

In their book *The Cry of the Soul*, authors Dan Allender and Tremper Longman III tackle the emotion of shame. Dr. Allender is well-known for his work with survivors of trauma and abuse and therefore has a lot to say about shame. In *The*

Cry of the Soul, human shame is identified as being corrosive in nature, and several signposts are given.

The first "signpost of shame" is absorption with self.[5] Indeed, when we struggle with shame, we tend to be very self-focused. We hurl vicious insults at our own worth and value. We identify with our shame. It seems to affect us down to the very core of who we are. As we wrestle with sin, we may find ourselves saying things like, "I'm so stupid. Why can't I figure this out? What is wrong with me? I'm so dirty and disgusting. I'm such a hypocrite."

The second signpost is flight from exposure. This is the idea of severing relationships. It's the response we see most prominently in the story of Adam and Eve. They are ashamed and so they hide. Never mind the fact God is omnipresent and omniscient. They still try to cover up. Shame drives us into hiding. It creates in us a need to escape.[6]

This is an especially dangerous aspect for those of us who struggle with sexual sin as a means of escape. If you're drawn to fantasy as a method of escaping life, you may feel shame for having that struggle. That shame increases your desire to hide, which, in essence, drives you back to and deeper into that fantasy world. In a twisted way, shame begets shame. Shame doesn't make you make good decisions. It makes you lie about the bad ones.

The third signpost of shame is violence, directed at ourselves or others or both.[7] This is the lashing out we may do to keep people at bay. It is almost a sense of anger meant to drive away and defeat the threat. We'll see this response in John 4. Unfortunately for us, the violence of shame is almost always aimed at the wrong target.

In my journey, I saw all three of these signposts as I struggled with an addiction to pornography and fantasy. When I tried to control my out-of-control porn use and realized I couldn't, shame overwhelmed me. *How did I get myself into this mess? What kind of monster have I become? There must be something wrong with me.* (Obsession with self.) I began to push people away, shut out relationships, and started pursuing even harder an image of being the "perfect Christian girl." The real me stayed hidden behind layers of people-pleasing and perfectionism. I did everything I could to keep from being found out. (Flight from exposure.)

As I wrestled through my struggle alone, I lashed out at others. In college, I attended mandatory anger management counseling to address the rage that consumed me. I had built walls around my heart, dug a moat, filled it with alligators, and then stationed fire-breathing dragons on top of the walls. If you dared to get close, I would be sure you didn't survive. I made it my goal to ensure no one would ever get in. (Violence.)

I wasn't just like this toward others, though. I also directed plenty of violence at myself. As a way of trying to gain control over my porn use, I resorted to self-harm. I thought, *If I can make this hurt, it will stop.* It seemed like a way out. In reality, it was another manifestation of the shame consuming my life.

The Blame for Shame

It's easy to blame my family or my church for my shame. After all, if my family had been willing to talk about sex or if my church hadn't been so legalistic, maybe I wouldn't have experienced what I did. If I had found a safe place to struggle, then maybe I would have come forward. But my experience with shame isn't unique. Women from amazing, open families attending grace-filled churches still struggle with shame. In fact, I've seen times where shame seems compounded in the lives of women who feel they have no reason or excuse for their struggle. If you come from a great, loving, godly, and safe home, you may feel even more shame that you struggle.

Allender and Longman explain shame, as we understand it in human terms, as ultimately an exposure of idolatry. They say, "Shame is not primarily an experience of feeling bad or deficient as it is the exposure of foolish trust in a god who is not God."[8] Shame reveals idols in our hearts, idols we're embarrassed to admit are there. That embarrassment and feeling of exposure are the roots of our shame.

My shame didn't come from the fact my family refused to talk about sex. It wasn't because of my legalistic church. My shame came from worshiping my own image of perfection. I worked hard to be the perfect student, the perfect Christian girl. After all, my grandfather served as a deacon. My grandmother taught Sunday school. My mom sang in the choir.

Long before I was exposed to pornography, I was obsessed with being perfect. Pornography threatened that perfection. Shame erupted from the thought of being exposed. My pursuit of perfection left me empty. It felt useless and foolish.

The worship leader who feels overwhelming shame because she struggles with pornography may be, in reality, worshiping her position and feels it is now at risk. The pastor's wife may be worshiping her status in the church and the image she has built of herself and her family. The missionary may be idolizing the praise of others for being "sold out" to God as she serves in a foreign land. The engaged woman may idolize her relationship and fear losing it if her sin is exposed. When our earthly idols are at risk of exposure and failure, we feel the sting of shame.

Shame Invites Grace

In contrast to the destructive human side of our shame that drives us into hiding and causes us to walk to wells at high noon, there is a holy element of shame too. If shame is an exposure of idols, then it is, in a sense, a way of drawing our hearts toward God. Shame and grace are unable to coexist, and yet, somehow, shame itself is an invitation to grace.

Let's revisit the story of Adam and Eve for a moment. In response to shame, they hid. They covered their nakedness (hiding from each other) and also hid from God. But how did God respond? He went looking for them.

In Genesis 3, God, knowing full well what had happened, calls out to them, "Where are you?" (v. 9). When Adam answers that he is hiding because he is naked, God's response is, "Who told you that you were naked? Have you eaten from the tree that I commanded you not to eat from?" (v. 11).

God extends the olive branch, if you will, a sense of reconciliation in response to their shame. He doesn't say, "Well, serves you right! You ought to be ashamed of yourselves!" Yet so often that is the voice we give God.

When the single woman who slept around years ago now can't find a husband, she imagines God is sitting in heaven punishing her. When the preacher's daughter is steeped in pornography and struggles to get out, she refuses to open her Bible because she thinks God is disgusted with her.

In our shame, we've painted this image of God that is all wrong. We've projected our shame onto him. God surely must be ashamed of us and so must exhibit all of the signposts of shame. He must be obsessed with what we've done wrong. He must not want anything to do with us at all, and he must be out to make sure we pay for what we've done. None of that is true. When we believe those lies of shame, we sour and sever the most important relationship in our lives.

Perhaps the most powerful piece of Scripture speaking against these lies is Psalm 139. This is a psalm of David—the David who killed Goliath and also raped Bathsheba and had her husband killed. In this psalm, David shares there is nowhere we can flee from God's presence, and we are known in our innermost being (vv. 1, 13). We are fearfully and wonderfully made (v. 14). And still, David calls God's thoughts precious and invites God to search his heart. This is not the song of a man overwhelmed by shame but a man who understands the love and mercy of God.

As we continue to explore this story of John 4, we'll see marks of shame in the Samaritan woman's life. You might be able to spot them in your own life. They'll manifest as desires you think are somehow wrong or defective, but they are desires God intends to meet and fill. He's not running from our shame; he's pressing into it and offering us grace. He's offering us himself and the opportunity to drop our idols and find satisfaction in him.

In the words of Allender and Longman,

> Brokenness is the antidote to shame. The power of shame is never crushed by affirming our goodness or dignity; instead, it is melted in sorrow when we are overwhelmed by what

it exposes in our hearts. . . . Sorrow, in turn, lifts our hearts before the One we have offended, in hunger for what seems inconceivable, given our condition: restored relationship. Any approach to shame that does not deepen our need for repentant sorrow will lead to a self-absorbed focus on ourselves rather than a greater confidence in grace.[9]

In your shame, have you lost sight of grace? Do you believe there's a way out, or do you feel stuck? Is your long walk driving you away from people or drawing you closer to God? These are all questions we have to answer for ourselves.

What is your long walk to the well? What areas of your life has shame reached out to touch? It might be your relationships with friends or family. It could be your job or your ministry. It may even show in your marriage or in how you parent your kids. You may see your long walk to the well as a punishment, as "the way things will always be."

Who knows how many days the Samaritan woman made that walk to that well. Who knows how many times she wished it could be different. On this day, things would change. Not because of anything she had done but because she met Jesus. Her shame had an encounter with grace, and grace changes everything.

CHAPTER 3

The Desire to Be Known

I tell people I have attended church since the Sunday before I was born. My family was composed of three generations of conservative Christians steeped in years of tradition, rules, and performance. People in church would tell us our behavior mattered, and we felt an unspoken pressure to put on the pretty face, suck it up, and perform for Jesus. Never talk back. Never speak out of turn. Never challenge the norm.

Even from a young age, I realized that the way we looked in public and how we were in private were two very different things. Many Sundays we were the family who yelled at each other the entire ride to church, sat still, smiled, and sang in service, and then fought the entire way home. At church and church events, we adhered to a specific standard of dress, speech, and action.

It went beyond typical social etiquette. We essentially censored what went on behind closed doors. We put on a mask along with our Sunday best. We believed this was what Jesus expected of us. Our best behavior. Our best clothes. Our best everything. Jesus didn't care about our brokenness. He simply demanded our absolute best. This resulted in years of brokenness disguised by plastered-on smiles and good church girl answers.

When I first started watching pornography at age thirteen, I didn't think to hide it. In my mind, using pornography was a perfectly acceptable alternative to sex. *Sex* seemed to be what people cared about. I figured that since pornography and masturbation weren't going to get me pregnant or give me an STD, they were fine. I never worried about things like clearing the browser history on the family computer. Until the day I was caught.

The conversation that ensued was filled with panic and desperation. I was asked why I was looking at pornography. "Please tell me you are just curious. Why are you looking at this?" To make it all stop, I said that curiosity was the only reason and I promised never to do it again.

That conversation did two things. First, it planted a seed of shame deep into my heart. I felt something must be wrong with me. Second, it threatened my safety. Not physically, but emotionally, mentally, and even spiritually. If this behavior was unacceptable, then I couldn't share it and I couldn't discuss it.

I promised outwardly that I would never look at pornography again but had no intention of keeping my word. Internally I promised I would never let myself get caught. So began the journey of shame in my life. I had an image to protect, and I must do it at all costs.

One morning, as a teenager, I sat at the table in my grand-parents' outdated dining room. Grampa occupied his usual seat near the back door, and I watched my Gramma working away furiously at the kitchen stove. The exact context of the conversation is lost now, but I will never forget the image of her turning from the stove, her tiny frame making her way across the green linoleum toward the table. She expressed her disgust for pornography and the people who watched it. "Those people are sick. Sick. Sick. Sick." With each "sick," she flicked the spatula in her hand for added emphasis.

I felt like a spy in my own family. A traitor.

I was one of "those people." I thought then, *If you really knew me, you wouldn't love me.* I worked even harder to keep up the façade. I volunteered in church youth group, helped my Gramma teach vacation Bible school, sang in competi-tions.

Living a Lie

Throughout the years of my struggle, with every accolade I re-ceived, every hug, every "I'm so proud of you," I just thought, *If you really knew who I am, you wouldn't love me. You wouldn't talk to me. You wouldn't want me.*

As sincere as people might have been, shame told me if they really knew me, they would change their minds. And so, nothing stuck. No praise mattered. No award satisfied. No amount of proclaimed love ever soothed my heart.

I wanted to hide and at the same time desperately wanted to be found out. I wanted to stop pretending. For years, I built up my image of a good church girl. I even submitted myself to the local newspaper as a model student and Christian.

They featured me in our small-town paper, highlighting how a recent mission trip to Mexico had "changed my life."

In a sense, I had created a picture-perfect me and did everything I could to be her. A living social media filter, if you will. Behind closed doors, I lived in a world filled with lust and porn. On the other side of those doors, I figured out expectations and worked hard to achieve them. I had to be perfect. The 4.0 student. The outspoken virgin. Decoy after decoy dispatched to ensure my secret world remained a secret. I did my best to model the "ideal" Christian woman, but only when others were watching.

It is an odd paradox to want to be known while also fearing it. I imagine that is what it must feel like to live "on the run." Constantly cleaning up after yourself. Constantly looking over your shoulder. Overthinking everything you say. Overanalyzing everything you do. Eventually, you just grow weary of running and sick of hiding. At least I did.

Living a double life is exhausting. It's a high pedestal to fall from, and the thought of jumping from it terrified me.

How do I start this conversation? It's not like I could just walk up to one of my aging pastors' wives and say, "Hi, I struggle with pornography." I feared the repercussions. What would happen to me? To my family?

I wanted to stop pretending I had it all together. At the same time, I did not know what would happen if people knew the truth. Would I lose everything? Would people walk away?

Fear of being known drove me deep into the shadows of shame. But we aren't made to live in the shadows. We are designed for the light of community. We are designed to be known—intimately, at that.

But if people knew the real me, the me who indulged in hours of hardcore pornography, the me who lied to cover it all up, the me who went out of my way to earn their trust and appear good, they wouldn't love me. I longed to be known and simultaneously feared it more than anything else. I fiercely protected the life and lie I had crafted.

A Simple Request

As the dialogue of Jesus and the Samaritan woman opens, Jesus has a simple request: "Give me a drink" (v. 7).

Place yourself in this story for a moment. Forget that we're talking about sexual sin here. Just imagine you're walking a path in your local park. You stop to take a swig of water out of your water bottle and, out of the corner of your eye, you notice an unassuming gentleman sitting on a nearby bench. He is obviously tired and has sat down to rest in the heat of the day. He says hello and asks if he can have a drink.

What would your initial response be?

If this scenario scares you and you're thinking, *Duh! I would run!* then, imagine, for the sake of safety, you are in a group.

What would your initial response be?

You may be shocked by his appearance or thrown by this unexpected plot twist in your day, but once that wears off, your response would probably be to find him something to drink. It's a simple request and easy to fulfill. If you question his motives, you may begin interrogating him, but if you feel safe and feel he is in need, why wouldn't you give him something to drink?

This is the scenario here at the well in John 4. Jesus is there. He is weary, and the woman has come there to get water. It is not out of her way or much extra work for her to help quench his thirst. But she doesn't.

Instead, her response is almost defensive.

> The Samaritan woman said to him, "You are a Jew and I am a Samaritan woman. How can you ask me for a drink?" (For Jews do not associate with Samaritans.) (v. 9)

She feels the need to set the record straight. She doesn't offer him water but instead challenges the nerve he has to ask her in the first place. She offers him a chance to abandon the conversation.

She points out the cultural boundaries Jesus is crossing, and there are several. Instead of welcoming the conversation of a stranger, she quickly corrects it. He shouldn't talk to her, and she lets him know it. This is not the response of a woman who feels safe. This is the response of someone who feels threatened.

Dr. R. Alan Culpepper writes that this encounter with the Samaritan woman crosses four different levels of tension: gender, nationality, race, and religion.[1] Here is a man. A *Jewish* man. A Jewish man in *Samaria*. A Jewish man *talking to a Samaritan*. A Jewish man talking to a Samaritan *woman*. Alone. By all accounts, this scenario should not be happening.

Some have pointed out that this clandestine meeting at a well is a type-story for marriage.[2] In other words, it's like the setup for an ancient-day fairy tale. Moses met his wife, Zipporah, at a well (Exod. 2). Isaac's wife, Rebekah, was found at a well (Gen. 24), and Jacob and his wife Leah met at a well (Gen. 29).

How's that for a twist? It's not just a meeting at a well but it has all the makings of a first-century romance.

If you're a young single woman who struggles with pornography and shame, imagine walking into church on a Sunday morning and going up to the coffee counter (assuming your church has one of those). You hear "Hi," turn around, and see a strapping young gentleman standing there, smiling at you. His smile is perfect. His voice is buttery. His eyes are glistening windows into his soul. It's like a scene from a low-budget Christian romance, and it's happening to you.

I'm happily married to an amazing man, and I can assure you this is not how it went down for us. Also, whose voice is "buttery"? But I remember those years of singleness and always hoping for the chance encounter.

If you're like me, you'd find such an encounter somewhat welcome and yet also very inconvenient. You might think to yourself, *Now is* not *a good time. Romeo, please come back later. I do not have the time or ability to deal with you today.*

I feel like that's the tone of this woman's response. For whatever reason, she wants nothing to do with this strange Jewish man hanging out near her well. She saddles him with the responsibility for the tension of this encounter. He is breaking the rules, and she reminds him of them.

The Walls We Build

Alone, shame leads us to believe, "If you really knew who I am, you wouldn't be talking to me right now." When someone does reach out in an attempt to talk to us and break through those walls of shame, it's not uncommon for us to lash out at them, as if they're the ones with the problem. Then the message changes to, "I don't *want* you to know who I am, so you shouldn't be talking to me right now."

Shame has a way of leaving us fearing the thing we want the most. In her book *The Emotionally Destructive Relationship*, counselor Leslie Vernick shares the story of Sara. Sara's father called her a whore throughout her childhood. When she was sixteen, tragically, a man raped her. In response, she started believing her father might be right. "She was no good. No decent man would be interested in her." When a Christian man did try to get to know her, Sara ghosted him. She explained her reasoning: "He would never be interested in me." As Vernick summarizes it, "She ran from him because she was afraid he'd reject her once he got to know her better."[3]

Perhaps you know this fear. When a young man says he wants to get to know you, you push him away, because you know you and believe he really *wouldn't* want to get to know you.

When your small group at church asks everyone for prayer requests, you would love to have the support of prayer. But you're petrified to speak the truth out loud. You mention an "unspoken need" and hang your head, worried that if they really knew, you would no longer be welcome. Or your college ministry asks everyone to take turns sharing their testimony, and your stomach turns. You write up a G-rated version of yours, reasoning that the struggles you have are too private for anyone to know.

This is one of the top concerns women share with me. They email me their stories of struggle, addiction, and frustration at their failure, and express relief in telling their stories to me. They are relieved that now somebody knows. When I respond that they really should tell someone who knows *them*, the response is almost always defensiveness and fear.

"I can't! I don't have anyone to tell. No one will understand. They will judge me." In some heartbreaking cases, they have told somebody but their fears have only been confirmed. They were shunned, ignored, treated like a leper.

We want to be known. At the same time, the prospect is terrifying because we don't know what happens next. When we build up a fake persona, when we pretend to be someone we're not, it's a bit like being a spy. The person receiving that love, earning those awards, having those relationships . . . she's not real. This leaves us both lonely and wanting to be left alone. We push people away because we don't want the truth to be known. If it is, we'll lose everything.

We settle for false connections to avoid the pain of having real ones. People in our lives easily accept a hologram of who we truly are. They love the filtered version of our lives, and we become dependent on those false connections and the false sense of acceptance they bring. We convince ourselves we can never lose the filter.

In a spiritual, emotional, and mental sense, we become like those people who go to a plastic surgeon asking to be made to look like they do on Snapchat. That's the image people have come to love. We feel we will lose all of the affection and attention if people find out who we really are, so we try to change who we are to fit the filter.

False Connections

All throughout high school, as I indulged in pornography, I worked hard to keep people away. When I finally wanted to get help, I had no idea how to do it. I started praying I would get caught, and it felt like a fierce grace in college when I did.

Finally, someone knew. As I read the email summoning me to the dean's office, relief, cautious hope, and terror seized my heart. Yes, finally someone knew, but I had no idea what they would do with this knowledge.

Would I get kicked out of school? Would they help me? Would they tell my family?

I listened as the dean talked about the evils of pornography. It reminded me of that moment in my Gramma's house when I heard about the sick people who indulged in it. This time felt different, though. The dean had hard evidence I could be identified as one of "those sick people." I couldn't get out of this one.

But then she said, "We know this wasn't you. Women just don't have this problem."

Even with a folder filled with evidence proving my guilt, she remained convinced this couldn't have been me because I was female. She explained the evidence away by accusing me of sharing my password with male classmates.

The "real me" had been exposed—I thought. Then, in a moment, I was completely ignored and invalidated. The dean had proof of the mask I wore, but she simply brushed it off and handed it back to me, along with a tube of superglue.

I didn't want to wear it anymore. I didn't want to play the games and keep on pretending. If I couldn't be the Christian girl who used to watch porn, I would be the porn star who used to be a Christian. Either way, the double life needed to end.

I threw myself into an online relationship with reckless abandon. I met a man in a chat room because those couldn't be traced. Up until this point, in chat rooms, I had always lied about who I was. I would give a fake name and lie about my height, weight, eye, and hair color. If a guy wasn't interested, I would leave the chat, go back in under a different name, and try again. This time was different. I gave him my real name, showed him my real picture, and gave him my log-in to my school's intranet.

He became the first person in the world to know the real me: a Christian girl who watched porn. He knew, and he accepted me. When he asked for nudes, I locked my dorm room door and gave him his pictures.

At seventeen years old, I let my desire to be known lead me to become someone else's pornography. When he responded, "You're beautiful," I would have done anything for him. He felt like the only person who could love me, because he knew me better than anyone else did. Or so it seemed.

This connection that felt so strong wasn't a connection at all. I had confused being known with being used. Instead of being loved as a person, I settled for being objectified as a commodity. The desire to be known had made me unknown.

Shame corrupts our desires with fear. Shame takes our desire to be known and tells us it is something to be afraid of. It attempts to kill that desire, leaving us disconnected, devoid of community and relationship. Essentially, shame wants us all to itself. It wants to run the narrative, and it will do so by convincing us that the way out is far too scary and basically impossible.

We fear the loss of any relationship and overwhelming judgment. To protect ourselves, we change who we are. We go out of our way to hide our failures, to mask our brokenness, to protect our weakness. We save face by painting a fake one, and as people fall in love with that face, we find our true selves starved of relationship.

The God Who Knows

Shame screams to our hearts, "God doesn't want to know you!" Think back to Adam and Eve in the garden. When they ate the fruit God instructed them not to, they realized their mistake. Their initial response was to hide. They fashioned some fig leaf garments to hide their nakedness, and then they hid their entire selves from God. They didn't just cover up; they tried to disappear.

Is that where you are?

On the one hand, you cover your tracks online. You are diligent to use a private browser, to clear your cache and search histories. You sew together your fig leaves. But beyond that, you hide from God. You keep your Bible closed. You don't pray because you feel like a hypocrite. You believe God doesn't want you. Shame has convinced you that you deserve exile, and so you have exiled yourself, slipping away quietly, hiding behind trees in the garden. You think God is disgusted with you. You think he wants nothing to do with you. You think, as you sneak away, that he is thinking, *Good riddance to bad rubbish.*

But on the other hand, look at God in the garden. God pursued. He came down and closed that gap. He went looking for Adam and Eve, knowing full well what they did. He knew, and he responded by pursuing them. He had all the power in the universe. He could have just blown the world up and started over. He could have just struck Adam and Eve dead where they stood and tried again. He could have walked away, abandoning humankind to its chosen demise.

God had an endless list of options for his response. He chose pursuit. He knew exactly what they did. Exactly what it would cost, both in their lives and in the course and history of humanity. He knew their decision would ultimately lead to the cross. And yet he pursued them, pressed into their need, and made a way for restoration (Gen. 3:14–15).

That is the same pattern we see at the well. Jesus knows the story of the woman he is talking to, and later this ends up being the testimony she takes back to her village. But for now, I want this truth to sink into your heart.

Jesus knows.

And that's not meant to be a judgmental, shame-inducing truth. I can't tell you the number of times I have heard pastors and leaders use that line to convince people to stop sinning. "Imagine Jesus is in the room with you watching that filth, because he is." Then they continue, "Imagine how sad that would make him." Hearing that only made me feel even more guilty about what I did. *Sorry, God, that I'm putting you through this.*

When I say Jesus knows, I don't want you to picture some almighty set of eyeballs glaring over your shoulder. I want you to picture a set of arms reaching for your heart. Because that's what God does. That's the entire message of the gospel. It isn't a frustrated, impatient God standing in heaven waiting for the world to get its act together. It is Immanuel, God made flesh, man of sorrows, acquainted with our suffering and our iniquity. He knows. He knows our temptations. He knows our weaknesses. He knows our pain and our woundedness. He didn't just come to us. He *became* like us (Heb. 2:17).

What happened to you at church camp? He knows. The wrong choices you made at that party? He knows. The frustration you feel when you fall yet again? He knows. The tears you cry, desperate for freedom and relief? He knows.

The number of times you've tried to stop entertaining those thoughts? He knows. The days you've felt like throwing in the towel? He knows. The times you've wondered if it really is so bad after all? He knows.

He knows you better than you know yourself. He knows your history, every wrong done to you, every wrong you have done. He knows every wound that has cut into your heart, every turn that has brought you to where you are. He knows the depth and darkness of your struggle. He sees your weariness and discouragement in fighting. He sees the days you binge on pornography without it even bothering you.

And while shame is telling you to run and hide, he knows—and he is coming for you. Not to bring judgment down on your head but to offer grace, freedom, and healing.

Some of us choose to hide from him by walking away from our faith, believing he wants nothing to do with us. We dive deeper into our struggles, give up fighting, and consider ourselves lost causes.

Others of us hide behind a good girl image. We go to church every Sunday, serve, carry our Bible to school. We lead Bible studies, always have the right answers, sing all the right songs. We talk a big Christian talk, but it's just a wall we're building. Maybe if we build it high enough, God will forget about what we're doing. Maybe he won't find us.

But he will. In fact, he never lost us for a moment. You can stop hiding from him. He already knows.

CHAPTER 4

The Desire to Be Free

So many Christians grow up with what I refer to as a "coloring page" approach to the Bible. Entire passages of biblical truth are reduced to one image, a craft, and a song. When we think of David, for example, we think of Goliath. Sunday school kids make little slingshots during craft time and sing about the giant falling down (conveniently leaving out the part where David chops off the giant's head).

In sermons, we refer to David as a man after God's own heart (1 Sam. 13:14). We preach about the five stones he used to kill Goliath and what those might represent. We may talk about how he played the harp for Saul or how he looked after sheep, but there aren't Sunday school coloring pages, crafts, or songs for David and Bathsheba. It's David and Goliath—that's the coloring page. One man's very complicated life journey, and God's involvement in that journey, reduced to the story of a shepherd boy anointed as king and defeating a giant with just a sling. The ultimate underdog.

For John 4, the coloring page is "Jesus is the living water." It's the subject of sermons, Sunday school songs, and happy hymns. We walk away with an image of a jug left at a well because Jesus is the living water. That's the takeaway, supposed to inspire us to leave our water jugs behind.

I'm not saying we need to read into every single Bible story. However, we miss layers of truth when we boil stories down to one takeaway point and a verse taken out of context. "Jesus is the living water." What does that even mean? The woman at the well didn't get it at first either.

At this point in the narrative, the conversation takes one of its many twists. This entire conversation is a volley of unexpected and atypical responses. After the Samaritan woman explains to Jesus he isn't supposed to be talking to her, he essentially counters her by saying she doesn't know who she is talking to either.

When first responding to Jesus, she says, "If you knew who I was, you wouldn't be asking me for water." He replies, and I paraphrase, "If you knew who I was, you would be asking me for water . . . but not just any water, living water" (v. 10).

This rightly confuses her.

> "Sir," the woman said, "you have nothing to draw with and the well is deep. Where can you get this living water? Are you greater than our father Jacob, who gave us the well and drank from it himself, as did also his sons and his livestock?" (vv. 11–12)

She looks at this weary Jewish man, alone and out of place, and begins to question his credentials. Just who does this stranger think he is, showing up in this foreign country making lofty claims about some special source of water? What is he talking about? After all, *he* is the one who asked *her* for water. If he had some super special secret water, why does he need her to give him a drink?

> Jesus answered, "Everyone who drinks this water will be thirsty again, but whoever drinks the water I give them will never thirst. Indeed, the water I give them will become in them a spring of water welling up to eternal life."
> The woman said to him, "Sir, give me this water so that I won't get thirsty and have to keep coming here to draw water." (vv. 13–15)

The Importance of Water

In a culture where we value water differently, it is easy for us to miss the significance of it in this story. When we can walk up to a sink, turn on a faucet, and have clean, filtered water, all of this back and forth about water, wells, and springs seems a bit boring. We are prone to skim right over it. But imagine being in a place where fresh, running water is not at your fingertips.

As I searched for a way to illustrate this significance, I thought back to my time in the Philippines, where I saw the importance and value of fresh, clean water. However, as I wrote this chapter, I also had my own personal, at-home experience with water.

The day before Thanksgiving, I hosted a retreat planning meeting at my home. I spent the morning doing laundry and washing the dishes before feeding my daughters lunch. After lunch, I cleaned up the baby, set her on the floor, and returned to the sink to wet a washcloth to clean off my toddler. I pulled up on the faucet I had just used. Nothing came out. As if it were some fluke, I lowered the handle and pulled up again, completely baffled. Not even a drop of water. Only then did I notice the line of four white utility trucks parked outside my house.

In a near panic, I bolted to the front door, pulled it open, and called to the maintenance worker clad in a bright orange vest who was walking across my front lawn. "Excuse me!"

No response.

A little louder this time, "Excuse me, sir!" He looked up at me. I called out to him, "We don't have any water?" I posed it as a question. I thought maybe they made a mistake. Maybe they had bumped something or turned something off in the course of whatever they were doing.

I can't say I'm the most rational in the initial moments of a perceived crisis.

"Yeah, sorry," he said. "We're trying to fix it. There's a leak up here, and we don't know how long it is going to take."

My mind immediately raced to dinner that evening and Thanksgiving the next day. How was I supposed to function without running water? I called my husband, interrupting a preaching meeting. Having no access to water threw me into a frenzy.

What should I do? Even though we live near hurricane territory, we don't make a habit of storing water in our house. We only had two cups of water in our teakettle. That was it. How do you prepare for dinner and Thanksgiving with two cups of water?

I watched as gallons of water sprayed out of a fire hydrant, turning my neighbor's yard into a swamp. More than once, I considered running out there and filling every container I could with water from that hydrant.

Because of my time in the Philippines, I realize just how many First World problems are in that scenario. It also revealed how much I take something like water for granted, even though I have stood among children covered in boils because they had no running water. Let's just say I am very used to having easy access to running water.

The word translated "living" in this passage is a verb meaning to be alive. When it is paired with "water," it doesn't mean that the water is alive but that it is flowing or moving.[1] It's a phrase used to describe a spring bubbling up or gushing out. This stands in contrast to the well water the woman came to draw.

Whenever I've read this story or any story about a well in the Bible, my mind has always pictured a wishing well. I imagine a hole dug straight down into the earth, with a little wooden pulley system set up on top. You hook up your bucket, lower it down with a rope, and haul it back up.

Not surprisingly, wells in Bible times weren't exactly that glamorous. Some wells were more like wide sets of stairs cut down to reach pools of water. The modern-day site known as Jacob's well is in the crypt of a Greek Orthodox church, Church of St. Photina, in the West Bank. (Tradition says that Photina was the name of the woman at the well.) The well found here is a very unassuming and quite literal hole in the ground over seven feet in diameter. Historians say it measured over a hundred feet deep.[2]

Can you imagine the amount of effort it would take to walk the half mile from town, lower your jug down into this well, haul twenty pounds of water up one hundred feet, and then carry that water back to town? This is no leisurely afternoon stroll to the vending machine. This is a necessary and intense activity.

Jesus's offer of a spring of water caught her attention, not because she understood it but because it sounded appealing. This conversation was happening at the well, as she was in the middle of her water-fetching routine. She was, in real time, aware of the intense work involved in getting water. If this stranger could give her running water, her life would be infinitely better. But she was completely missing his point.

Sometimes we get the wrong ideas about freedom.

What Jesus Is Offering

As Bible readers with the whole story, we understand Jesus isn't offering an actual spring of water. We realize the offer Jesus makes in this passage is one of eternal life. He is offering the "gift of God" to the woman at the well. However, she takes him literally. Studying her misunderstanding is an important part of this story because we tend to misunderstand his offer as well.

When Jesus speaks of the water he intends to give, he twice mentions thirst. "Everyone who drinks this water will be *thirsty* again, but whoever drinks the water I give them will never *thirst*" (vv. 13–14).

He offers water to quench thirst. There's nothing fancy in the Greek here; he uses the word that means to be thirsty. However, we understand this to be metaphorical. Jesus does not intend to quench her literal thirst. He means a deeper, more spiritual thirst. We see this explained later, when Jesus stands up in a crowd and calls out, "If anyone thirsts, let him come to me. . . . As the Scripture has said, 'Out of his heart will flow rivers of living water'" (John 7:37–38 ESV). In that passage, we see he is referring to the Holy Spirit.

This isn't an uncommon tactic for Jesus. He often speaks in parables, metaphors, and riddles. In John 3, a Pharisee and member of the Jewish ruling council, Nicodemus, comes to Jesus at night. In their discussion, Jesus tells Nicodemus that only those who are "born again" can see the kingdom of God (John 3:3). This confuses Nicodemus, and he asks how this is even possible. Nicodemus can't wrap his mind around the thought of someone crawling back inside their mother's womb. Speaking as a mom of two, I can say I am most grateful this is not what Jesus means. Jesus goes on to explain he doesn't mean a literal rebirthing but a figurative/spiritual one.

In John 2, Jesus dramatically clears a pop-up shop out of the temple, offending the Jewish leaders. When the Jews challenge his authority, he tells them they could destroy the temple and he would raise it back up. It confuses them. After all, it took forty-six years to build it! Who does this person think he is? How could he rebuild it in three days? But Jesus doesn't mean the literal temple. Instead, he means his own body, which will be destroyed in the crucifixion and then raised back up again (v. 21).

Jesus often uses a physical scenario to explain a spiritual truth as a way of grabbing people's attention. In response, his listeners become confused. That confusion then allows him to explain what he means and, often, point out flaws in their thinking. This encounter with the woman at the well is no different. While we know his offer to quench her thirst is metaphorical, she does not.

When we look at her response, we see her misunderstanding. She wants to take Jesus up on his offer—who wouldn't? But notice what she adds. She wants this water so she will no longer thirst *and no longer have to come to the well to draw water* (v. 15).

Jesus offers water to quench her thirst, but he never mentions she won't have to come back. *She* adds that. She misinterprets what he is trying to give her.

A quenched thirst wouldn't stop her need for water. She would still need water for cooking, cleaning, and laundry. Her interest in Jesus's water is not primarily in relieving her thirst. She wants it so she will no longer have to come to the well.

He is offering satisfaction for her soul. She hears an offer for indoor plumbing. If her walk to the well every day represents and cements her identity in shame, she is asking Jesus to take it away. She sees his offer not as a way out of thirst but as a way to avoid shame. She doesn't want quenched thirst; she wants more convenient water.

False Freedom

This is the approach so many of us take to freedom. Instead of true freedom, we want freedom from feeling bad about our choices. We think freedom is being able to live exactly as we choose without anyone judging us for it. We want indoor plumbing. We want God to drill a pipeline of life right into our pit of death.

I should be able to watch pornography and not feel guilty.
So what if I'm sleeping around? Don't judge me.
What's the big deal about lust? If men can, why can't women?
Shouldn't women be free to express themselves sexually however they want? Shouldn't women be empowered?
Why is God telling me what to do with my sexuality?

If you've never heard her story, I'd like to introduce you to Mo Isom Aiken. She is a wife, a mom of four, and a woman who has walked this journey to the well. She has written some amazing books on sexual freedom and Christ, including *Sex, Jesus, and the Conversations the Church Forgot* and *Fully Known: An Invitation to True Intimacy with God.*

In *Fully Known*, she shares,

> We chose, and often continue to choose, our own desires because they are falsely disguised as freedom, an offer of "singleness." We desire autonomy and take the bait, but we fail to realize we are actually being trafficked, enslaved by sin. We leave our Father's house to live in the brothel of a fallen world presently governed by an abuser.[3]

It's a powerful word picture for us to consider. In my experience, we tend to choose "the brothel" for one of two reasons. We either like it there or feel like we cannot leave.

Freedom for many of us means we want to be free to choose whatever we would like without feeling guilty. What we don't realize is the pursuit of that freedom can drive us into isolation. If we feel our families are too strict, we leave. If we feel the church is too judgmental, we find a new one or walk away from God altogether. We surround ourselves with people who will not make us feel bad about our choices. We want to keep doing what "comes naturally" without feeling bad about it, but the reality is, as Galatians 5:17 says, "the flesh desires what is contrary to the Spirit, and the Spirit what is contrary to the flesh. They are in conflict with each other, so that you are not to do whatever you want."

We don't want to be judged, and everyone knows God is "judgy."

There is some bittersweet truth to this. The church, for quite some time, has mishandled sexuality, burying it under shame and expecting it to pop out unscathed after we say "I do." In many Christian circles, questions are silenced, and sex is a topic only addressed negatively. *Don't have sex before marriage. Don't watch porn. Dirty. Bad. Gross.* It's this flawed, shame-based messaging that has fueled a great number of stories of "deconstruction" or "exvangelicals." Listen to the stories and you will likely hear them talk specifically about how the church talks (or doesn't talk) about sex.

Messages of sex being dirty, wrong, or gross quickly lose their power when we begin to experience sexual pleasure. Then we have to reconcile our desires with our faith. Often our faith starts to lose. We struggle to justify our pursuit of that pleasure—a pursuit leading us away from pleasure as it was originally intended to be. We want our guilty pleasure without the guilt.

Casey wrestled with pornography and masturbation for years. She had difficulty reconciling this struggle with her faith and reached out to talk. As I do with almost every woman who contacts me, I encouraged her to reach out to people in her community instead of fighting on her own. She would not, fearing that they would judge her and disown her. So I encouraged her to pray for God to bring someone to her. She then told me she didn't even want to pray because she was convinced God hated her and wouldn't even listen to her anyway.

We corresponded for a few months before she sent her final email. In it, she told me she had given up on God and church, met an older man who "loved her," and they "had sex all the time." She shared she had never been happier, had left her church and her family, and now lived with this man. She settled for a different kind of freedom—ultimately destroying every relationship she had—for the sake of experiencing sexual pleasure.

We're settling for the same old water, the same old thirst, but asking for indoor plumbing. *Pipe it straight to me, in my home. Let me enjoy my water in peace.* And we call that freedom.

We choose our own desires because that choice feels like freedom. We want God's stamp of approval for this, but God realizes something we don't. This "freedom" is poison. It is deadly. It is no freedom at all. Just like pornography can take our desire to be known and try to satisfy it with false connections, our desire for freedom can be twisted. We settle for what looks like freedom, but it is not real.

We realize this too late. Once the lights fade and the glitter wears off, we tire of life in "the brothel." We head for the door. Believing we've been free this whole time, we assume we're also free to leave. That's when we come face-to-face with the abuser. That's when our own bodies and shame turn on us, order us back to our rooms, and lock the door.

Is Freedom Possible?

Many women who struggle with sexual sin want freedom. We just don't know how it's possible. Feeling hopeless, we can hide behind words like *addiction* and tell ourselves it's not our fault, and we can never be free. We're afraid even if we do somehow get "free," we will never know life without the weight of shame. The future seems like it will be filled with labels, judgment, and dead ends. We feel we can never have unhindered intimacy and healthy relationships.

In my journey, freedom often felt out of reach. My exposure to pornography happened innocently enough—just a stray video while researching for school. Within a few years, it became unmanageable. What started as curiosity grew into a hobby and then morphed into a compulsion that began to control my life. By the time I graduated from high school, pornography, masturbation, and lust were second nature.

A pastor once said to me, in passing, "I've never heard of a woman spending hours a day watching porn." Whether he had ever heard of it or not, that's precisely what I did. Some days I would wake up in the morning and say, "Not today. I will *not* use porn today." But without fail, I would find myself back at the computer, logging on to the same sites. In desperation, I enabled parental controls. But because I knew the password, I would just override the controls.

Getting rid of pornography didn't look like a possibility. It felt as though I'd already gone too far. I'd already messed up too much. No life existed without pornography. I might as well embrace it.

That message grew in strength after I was caught in college and then dismissed because "women don't have this problem." As I mentioned in the last chapter, after that meeting, I gave up. I sent nudes to a guy I met online. Then I dropped out of college.

I spent months trying to figure out how to apply for work on porn sites. For me, being able to fully embrace this part of me spelled freedom. My double life had gotten old. I searched desperately for freedom—freedom from pretending.

I never did figure out how to apply for work on porn sites. Thankfully, at that time it wasn't as easy as applying for a job at the local mall. In those months after leaving college and wrestling with what freedom looked like, I realized I didn't want a life without God in it somehow. I decided to attend Bible college the following fall, but I still didn't have any idea what freedom looked like.

As I prepared to go off to Bible college, I tried to make a deal with God. I prayed, "God, I will follow you, but you have to understand this addiction comes with me. I will serve you and love you, but this has to stay. I've tried to beat it and I can't. Sorry."

In my mind, plenty of pastors struggled with pornography and still did great work. I had also heard of missionaries who struggled with it and still served God. Therefore I could be a Christian girl who struggled with pornography. To me, that felt as close to freedom as I would ever get.

For some people, that watered-down version of freedom feels good enough. It's facing in the right direction—but it still isn't freedom. It's like looking the other way in a jail cell. Turn one way, and you're looking at the dark and cold of the jail hallway. Turn the other way, and you're staring out the window. Either way, you're still stuck. Either way, you're not free. Even if you're walking around without chains, if you're still in the cell, you're not free.

It might *feel* like freedom to do whatever you want without stigma or shame. It might *feel* like freedom to cut yourself off from everyone who is "judging" you. You might get angry with people who tell you what you're doing is wrong and surround yourself with people who support your decisions. You may even say they "accept" you. They "love" you, and that seems like freedom. But it isn't.

The offer of Christ isn't water piped straight to where we are.

Jesus isn't offering us indoor plumbing. He wasn't offering it then, and he's not offering it now. His offer is not to save us from our need for water. He's not offering to stamp approval on our ways. He's offering us a better way.

The God Who Frees

We have to be careful not to settle for false freedom.

Is true freedom from a struggle with sexual sin possible? Yes.

It's not only possible, it's exactly what God desires for us. But we don't often view the gospel as a fight for our freedom.

Throughout the Bible, we read about God's desire for freedom. "It is for *freedom* that Christ has set us free. Stand firm, then, and do not let yourselves be burdened again by a yoke of slavery" (Gal. 5:1). "For the law of the Spirit of life has *set you free* in Christ Jesus from the law of sin and death" (Rom. 8:2 ESV).

The gospel is about freedom—freedom from sin, freedom from our struggles, freedom even from our out-of-control desires. With that also comes freedom from shame and condemnation, which is what many of us are hoping for.

Admittedly, plenty of Christians disconnect these applications of freedom. On the one hand, some emphasize that the gospel frees us from our sin but neglect that it also intends to free us from our shame. They believe in freedom from sin and believe God can set people free from struggle, but they continue to hold on to shame. They keep struggles and sin quiet and silence recovered sinners, not allowing them to share their stories or how God has worked in their lives. The single mom who got pregnant out of wedlock years ago isn't allowed to sing in the choir. The former opioid addict isn't allowed to share his story of redemption. The former porn addict or girl who sent nudes isn't allowed to speak to teenagers for fear she will "rob their innocence" or plant ideas in their heads.

It's no wonder we struggle with finding hope for freedom when it seems there is more shame in freedom than in our struggle itself! If the future looks dark, it's hard to have hope. But without hope, we won't fight for freedom.

That kind of shame-tainted freedom is not what God wants for us. His desire is for us to know no condemnation (Rom. 8:1). His desire is for us to know abundant life and freedom from sin *and* shame. He wants to quench our thirst with living water and rid us of the shame we feel from our struggle.

On the other hand, some embrace the gospel's message of freedom from shame while ignoring the freedom from sin it gives us. This is the "don't judge me" crowd. These people act like God's love and the gospel are nothing more than a license to live however we want. They are quick to remind others that there is no condemnation while also ignoring the Bible's repeated calls to honor God with our lives.

The freedom God offers is not the freedom to do whatever we want. The freedom he offers us is a release from slavery to our own out-of-control desires. It's a freedom from what the Bible calls the slavery of sin (Rom. 6:20). When we decide the freedom we want is "indoor plumbing," it falls far short of the comprehensive deliverance Christ offers.

God desires to liberate us from our longing for things that don't satisfy. The freedom of the gospel is not watching porn without shame; it's being liberated from the need to watch porn and from the shame of having once watched porn. It's not freedom to lust without inhibition; it's freedom from the traps of lust.

The freedom God offers releases us from our past mistakes, our present struggles, and our future shame. He is not offering to pump water straight to us so we can hide and stay where we are. He is offering us better water.

CHAPTER 5

The Desire to Be Loved

A t this point in John 4, the conversation shifts. It started with Jesus asking the Samaritan woman for water. She didn't offer it. Then he offered her water. She asked for it, not fully understanding what Jesus was implying, but he didn't give it. Now, in a seeming change of subject, he asks her to call her husband. In a bit of a conversational dance, he says, "'Go, call your husband and come back.' 'I have no husband,' she replied" (vv. 16–17).

This may seem like a bizarre way to continue the conversation, but it harks back to the beginning of the dialogue. Her first response to Jesus's request was intended to remind him of who she thought he was—a Jewish man who should not be asking her for a drink. Now, his response to her request for water reminds her of who she is.

He asks her to bring her husband.

Different Bible teachers have different viewpoints on why the conversation progresses this way. Some believe it would have been an entirely appropriate response. While women frequently were the water carriers, sometimes men would carry larger amounts of water. Jesus could be implying that she's going to need some help hauling this water back.[1]

It's also possible Jesus changes the subject as his way of getting to the point. It's as if he's saying, "Ok, you're not getting the subtle hint; let me just cut to the chase."

Whatever motivated the shift, the outcome is the same. The woman reveals that she does not have a husband.

As I reflected on this story years ago, this part spoke so tenderly to my heart. Jesus is pressing into her need. She asked for the water because she wanted to be done with the shame, loneliness, and isolation. She wanted the symptoms to be numbed. Jesus gently and adeptly bypasses that and goes right for the root of the issue. He points out her pain.

I'd imagine this felt like the end of the line for her. One moment she thinks she is going to have this living water. She is going to be able to be done with all of her shame. She lays down her defensive interrogation of Jesus and decides to take him up on this water. There is hope.

Then, the next moment, she has to reveal who she is. The mask is going to come off, and instead of finding freedom from her shame, she is going to have to reveal the very thing causing it.

In my mind's eye, I picture her shoulders slumping, her face turning away, and her voice lowering as she quietly says, "I have no husband." When I put myself in her place, I imagine thinking, *Well, there goes that offer. What a waste of time. I should have known better than to hope any differently.*

Have you ever been there?

Maybe you've sat in church and heard all about how God so loved the world. Grace, forgiveness, and unconditional love sound amazing. Then you hear part of the process involves "confessing your sins," and you think that will be the end of the line. Unconditional love sounds nice on paper, but you are almost certain the offer doesn't apply to you. There's no way God could love you like that. Perhaps love has always cost you something.

In their book *Free to Thrive*, authors Josh McDowell and Ben Bennett outline seven longings we each have: acceptance, appreciation, affection, access, attention, affirmation of feelings, and assurance of safety.[2] When you group these seven longings together, it paints a fairly accurate picture of what love looks like practically.

If we're honest, this isn't the love many of us experience on a day-to-day basis. Lust, abuse, and selfishness all masquerade as love, even claiming to be done in the name of love. But they aren't love; they are counterfeits. They are bullies. In my devotional *Love Done Right*, I call these "broken loves."

We experience broken love when our parents or spouse abuse us. We are wounded by broken love when we suffer abandonment or divorce. We live in an exploitive culture where love is based on performance instead of personhood. We love and lose, only to love again and be hurt.

We start to feel like love has a price tag. Something that should be unconditional becomes a status that must be earned. As much as we want it, it's not worth the cost. So we settle for false loves. The fake friendships, the one-night stands, the fans and follows on social media. True connection is too costly. It's not worth it.

In *The Sacred Romance*, authors Brent Curtis and John Eldredge write,

> We can either deaden our heart or divide our lives into two parts, where our outer story becomes the theater of the should and our inner story the theater of needs, the place where we quench the thirst of our heart with whatever water is available.[3]

The problem is, not all water is good water.

False Loves

Did you know ocean water can kill you? Even though it is water, its salt content is so high that drinking it will cause your body to release the water it already has in it to dilute the salt in the water you are drinking. This is quite literally the opposite of having your thirst quenched. Instead of giving water to your body, saltwater pulls water *out* of your body.

This is how desires are deadened. Jay Stringer is a licensed mental health professional specializing in unwanted sexual behavior. In his book *Unwanted*, he warns, "When we condemn our God-given desire to be loved and accepted, we should be on high alert for ways we will trash this longing through shameful behavior."[4]

This strategy of simply deadening our hearts to our desire for love also becomes a problem when we have to face God's love. His love seems almost impossible. Too good to be true. As we look at it, shame hisses in our ears, "What's the catch?" Just like pornography offers false connections to fill our desire to be known and false freedom to satisfy our desire to be free, we can find a false love to assuage our desire to be loved.

When the Samaritan woman admits she doesn't have a husband, Jesus responds that he knows this already. He then reveals his knowledge that she's had five husbands. On top of that, the man she is with now is not her husband.

Like a surgeon draining an abscess, Jesus asks a seemingly misplaced question that breaks open the source of her hurt. He exposes the area of her life in need of living water.

The area of your life where you experience the most shame is likely the area in need of the most grace. When reflecting on this passage, Dr. Juli Slattery says,

> Jesus knew how to get to this woman's heart. Endless hours of discussing the Jewish law and the theology of worship would have done nothing to change her life. But when the conversation turned personal, her need for healing and love became front and center.[5]

This entire time she'd been protecting this part of who she was. If he really knew she had five husbands and was with a man who wasn't her husband, he surely wouldn't have been talking to her. Instead of withdrawing his offer, though, Jesus reveals the truth he knew all along. The thing she thought for sure would disqualify her from the offer made no effect on the offer.

As Jay Stringer points out, "The gospel teaches us that we are beloved before any sexual sin or addiction entered into our lives, and we remain so, even at the height of our brokenness."[6]

Choosing Love

I truly believe lives would be changed if we began to understand the gospel and God's love the way God intended. So many of us have grown up in Christian cultures filled with messaging centering on our identity as something just above scum. We are peons in God's society.

Even when we hear about the gospel and God's love for the world, it is cast in such a way that he had to save us from our sorry selves. He is an angry, impatient, frustrated God who just wants us to hurry up and get our acts together. When we sin, we are told it's just like nailing Jesus to the cross again.

Shame has even slithered its way into our conversations about God's love! We believe our identity as new creations depends on whether or not we *act* like new creations. We believe our status as beloved depends not on God's gift of love but instead on whether or not we are *acting* like we're beloved. When we watch pornography, we aren't acting like we're loved, therefore we believe God couldn't possibly love us. He'll love us when we act like something he would want to love.

With shame writing the story, love is not a conscious choice and covenant but instead a status we must earn and keep. Shame tells us we must pay to be loved. The danger we run into is casting God to be an abusive, heartless dictator. He is demanding and unsafe, ready to respond in anger to our failure instead of being a loving Creator who sacrificed much to love us and loves us even when we are our most "unlovable."

If you doubt that, reflect on Romans 5:8–10. There, you will see that God proves his love for us in that "While we were still sinners, Christ died for us" (v. 8). While we were doing absolutely nothing worthy of love, we received the love of God, and this act of love justifies us and saves us from God's wrath.

Do you get it? *Even while you are messing up,* God makes a way for you to know the fullness of his love. It's all on him. *He* loves. *He* sacrifices. *He* justifies.

What are *you* doing while he does all of this? You are sinning. Still, he makes a way for you to know him.

We have a choice. We can choose to believe we are redeemed women who choose to sin. Or we can choose to believe we are dirty, rotten, no-good sinners who struggle with sin and will never be free. If you're honest, you'll admit you're likely living as if the second one is the truth.

Instead of letting our struggle dictate how we interpret God's love, we need to reverse it and let God's love dictate how we view our struggle. And that struggle is primarily with the *temptation* to sin. When we open up the internet browser and pull up our go-to porn site, we're beyond the "struggle" phase.

In James, we read about the life cycle of sin: "But each person is tempted when he is lured and enticed by his own desire. Then desire when it has conceived gives birth to sin, and sin when it is fully grown brings forth death" (1:14–15 ESV). The first line of battle is not with sin itself but with our desires.

We thirst. Then we have to decide what to do with that thirst. God offers us living water. He offers us perfect love. Yet we often choose lesser loves.

The Power of Confession

When we give in to temptation, that's sin. We try to soften it by calling it a "failure" or "falling" or "slipping." But this isn't an ice-skating rink. This is life. We aren't helpless victims of some force beyond our control. In our moments of "falling" or "slipping up," we are choosing to sin.

That is simply seeing it the way God sees it. This is what it means to confess.

When the woman at the well reveals she does not have a husband, Jesus seems to applaud her for telling the truth. "Jesus said to her, 'You are right when you say you have no husband. The fact is, you have had five husbands, and the man you now have is not your husband. What you have just said is quite true'" (John 4:17–18).

I think when we hear *confession*, our brains automatically jump to a true-crime documentary. We picture the cold interrogation room with the uncomfortable metal chairs, the good cop and bad cop sitting across from us, and an unopened water bottle just begging us to share some DNA. They present the evidence, pound their fists on the table, and ask questions. We confess, and then we get hauled off in cuffs to do our time.

That is not the biblical model of confession. In 1 John 1:9, we're given a beautiful promise: "If we confess our sins, he is faithful and just to forgive us our sins and to cleanse us from all unrighteousness" (ESV).

The word translated "confess" here doesn't mean to spill the beans but rather to speak the same thing. Confession isn't "turning ourselves in"; it's calling our actions what they already are. The first step is to stand with God and tell it like it is. Call it what it is. He calls it sin. It doesn't mean he doesn't acknowledge the struggle. He does. But when we give in to temptation, we're missing the mark he has for us. We're sinning.

We've all done it; you aren't alone. The pastor in your church, your Bible study leader, your spouse, your kids, your best friend, your favorite worship leader, the sixty-year-old church organist. All of us have sinned. That's a cornerstone of the gospel. That's one of those statistics God cares about.

When we stand with God and recognize that, when we say, "God, I know I have sinned. I know that I gave in to temptation. I looked at that website again and I know that violates your design for sex. I know that is wrong, short of your glory, and offensive," we set it up for him to take the next step.

Step 1: we confess.

Step 2: he forgives.

There isn't a Step 1.5 where he has to think about it. Or one that says he will first make us do community service. There is no step where he storms off mad and refuses to forgive us until he cools down.

We confess. He forgives.

The Greek word for "forgive" here means to send away or to release. Shame tells us we're trapped in our sin. God's forgiveness releases us from it.

First John 1:9 also tells us that God is faithful to forgive. He is loyal to this. This is part of who he is. It is what he does.

Not only is he faithful but he is also just.

I have known this verse for decades, but it is only recently that the word "just" stood out to me. The verse could say, "He is faithful to forgive our sins" and that would be enough. Why does it also mention God is just?

The Greek here is the same word translated "righteous." It's a callback to God's character. He is faithful to forgive, and he is right to forgive. It is within his character and his power to release us from our sins.

But the layers keep coming. Not only is he faithful and just to release us from our sin but he also cleanses us. This is what I love about grace. It would have been enough for God to just rescue me from my sin and save me from my struggle. I would have been totally happy with that. I just wanted out of the brothel. A cardboard box on the street would have been fine. I just wanted to escape.

I think that's what a lot of us are willing to settle for, "God, just make this stop. That's all I want. I just want this to stop. I don't care about anything else."

You might not care about anything else—but he does.

The word translated "cleanse" here means to make pure. Isn't that what we want? Isn't that what we're searching for? Release from sin and a slate wiped clean?

Let's put this all together. We call our sin what it is. We agree with God on it, and he will faithfully and righteously release us from its hold and its sentence on our lives. Not only that but he himself will do the work of cleansing us from all unrighteousness. He—not our works, not our cool strategies, not our hundred-day porn-free streak—will purify us.

Shame wants you to believe you are stuck. Dirty. Shame will tell you that you've essentially taken a bath in permanent ink. You are scarred for life. Shame will tell you that getting clean is your job, and it will have you hiding in the corner for the rest of your life, scrubbing away like Lady Macbeth. You've lost your chance, and you'll never live this down.

But that's not grace. Grace levels the playing field. We're all sinners. We have all messed this up, and we all do things that offend a holy God. The only way any of us experience freedom from that is through Jesus and through this act of confessing and allowing God to do his work.

Do you know what this means? This means no matter how "dirty" we are when we walk into 1 John 1:9, we're all the same level of clean coming out of it.

How Porn Destroys Love

Perhaps you feel like you aren't actually looking for love. You feel very loved and connected. Those seven longings mentioned at the beginning of this chapter are all met. You view your struggle as purely sexual. But what if I were to tell you what you believe about sex reflects what you believe about God's love for you? Would you think that was a bit of a stretch?

In the Bible, human sexual love is used as a picture of divine love. In Ephesians 5, Paul, a single man, scratches the surface of this mysterious connection. The sexual union parallels God's love for the church. If we believe that to be true, then we have to deal with what that means for things like pornography.

Pornography is sex on display for entertainment. Arguably the most intimate act any two people can partake in is viewed by hundreds of thousands of people. It is scripted, reduced to performance, cut, redone. People watch and achieve their own sexual release without relationship, without love.

Pornography conveys the message that sex and love are divorced. Disconnected. One does not lead to or need the other. You can have sex without loving the person. You can have sexual release without knowing the person. This is the argument of pornography and even, in a broader sense, culture in general. You can experience the *pleasures* of "intimacy" without actual intimacy.

When we let this mindset settle into our hearts, we struggle to grasp the idea of God desiring a relationship with us. In *Fully Known*, Mo Aiken shares,

> When we are tempted to watch porn for entertainment and arousal, we are feeding off the rush of viewing an act that God designed to be intimate and hidden. . . . This deeply perverts our understanding of true intimacy with God, because not only is our perception of intimate exchange seen through a perverted, evil, and lascivious lens but we also begin to retire to spiritual viewership, convinced that solely looking upon someone else's spiritual intimacy through their revelation and teaching and packaged presentation is a good-enough version of the real thing.[7]

If this is what you believe, then you may feel you show God your love by going to church, even by reading your Bible. You are displaying your devotion as if God wants to be entertained by your walk. You may listen to the Christian podcasts and have the best and latest worship playlist. But if God doesn't have your heart, he doesn't have you. He isn't interested in your performance. He wants you to know him, to experience him and the fullness of life he has for you. He wants intimacy with you, and when you experience that intimacy and that love, you easily recognize a counterfeit.

The God Who Loves

The Bible tells us nothing we do can separate us from God's love.

> No, in all these things we are more than conquerors through him who loved us. For I am sure that neither death nor life,

nor angels nor rulers, nor things present nor things to come, nor powers, nor height nor depth, nor anything else in all creation, will be able to separate us from the love of God in Christ Jesus our Lord. (Rom. 8:37–39 ESV)

Shame keeps many of us from reaching out and finding help for fear we may lose the love we already have. Even though love is one of the basic needs we have as image-bearers of God, even though it is one of the callings we have as Christians, shame makes us believe we are incapable of being loved. And if we are not capable of being loved, we will have a difficult time loving others.

If you struggle to love well in your human relationships, this might be part of the reason why. Later in the book of John, Jesus tells his disciples that they have a new commandment to love one another just as he has loved them (13:34). This is similar to the charge in Ephesians 5 for husbands to love their wives "as Christ loved the church" (v. 25). God's love for us is a blueprint for how we are to love others.

In 1 John 4, we see that God doesn't just love us; he *is* love.

Dear friends, let us love one another, for love comes from God. Everyone who loves has been born of God and knows God. Whoever does not love does not know God, because God is love. This is how God showed his love among us: He sent his one and only Son into the world that we might live through him. This is love: not that we loved God, but that he loved us and sent his Son as an atoning sacrifice for our sins. Dear friends, since God so loved us, we also ought to love one another. No one has ever seen God; but if we love one another, God lives in us and his love is made complete in us. (vv. 7–12)

When I understand God's love for me, I am able to love others well. However, if I believe that God's love is contingent on my behavior or that there are strings attached, and conditions, I will love others the same way. If I believe God secretly holds my sins against me, then I will hold things against others. What I believe about God's love for me is going to be reflected in how I give love to and receive love from others.

To borrow a phrase from *Sexual Sanity for Women*, "God's offer of home, unlike people or sex, provides what is truly secure, continual, comforting, peaceful, and profoundly intimate."[8]

The woman at the well didn't know it, but the love she had been looking for literally stood right in front of her. The same holds true for us. We are on a search for acceptance, intimacy, and unconditional love, and we look for it in so many places. In a world of broken and false loves, in a culture that tells us the only love that matters is our love for self, the love we have been looking for has been standing in front of us all along.

CHAPTER 6

The Desire to Worship

At this point, you may be thinking, *This doesn't sound like anything special. I've heard this all before.* That's because this is what Christians know as the gospel, and it is the same for everyone, regardless of what you have or have not struggled with.

The gospel is God's answer for a lost and dying world that has been wounded by brokenness and ensnared in sin. Earlier I shared that the only statistics that matter to God are all, none, and everyone. God's solution to all who have sinned and none who are righteous is that everyone who calls on his name will be saved. As a woman trapped in pornography, you don't have to sneak through a special back door to get to Jesus.

But if the gospel is the same for everyone, then where is the disconnect for you? You believe all of this, so why isn't it "working"? The testimonies we showcase on stage often make it sound like we believe God's love for us, believe the gospel, and then everything changes in an instant. *Suddenly* addictions are broken. *Suddenly* prisoners are set free. *Suddenly* we stop cursing, stop doing drugs, stop thinking bad thoughts. The process of sanctification appears to be instantaneous. When we don't experience such a sudden change in our lives, we can feel broken.

I felt like this the day after I got married. I don't know what I expected to happen, but I thought I would wake up and feel like a "wife." Instead, I felt like me. My status had changed and my responsibilities had changed, but I had not suddenly changed. I felt the same. My life was just different. And adjusting to it was a process. I had to learn how to live with my husband. I became a wife on paper in just a moment, but living out that reality remains a day-by-day journey of growth.

This is the case with our Christian walks as well. You might go to church on Sunday, read your Bible, and pray, all with the hopes that something magical will happen. Then it doesn't. You feel the same old temptation, visit the same old sites, and feel the same old guilt and shame. You conclude that you must not be loving Jesus hard enough, and your solution is that you just need to try harder. When you feel like you've tried everything and tried as hard as you can and it still doesn't work, the only thing left for you to think is that God has given up on you.

An author recently posted about a book he'd written on pornography (for men), and a perhaps well-intentioned commenter made the argument that real men who love Jesus don't watch pornography. If they really truly loved Jesus, then they wouldn't take part in this filth. To some extent, that commenter was right. At the moment we sin, we are choosing to love something other than Jesus.

But that's true for anyone and any sin, not just sexual struggles. Let's take that same logic and apply it to other seemingly mundane sins. "If you really loved Jesus, you wouldn't struggle with road rage." "If you really loved Jesus, you wouldn't struggle with envy."

Let's set the record straight: our churches are *filled* with people who struggle to love Jesus all of the time. But we're also really good at faking it.

This creates a problem for those of us who sit in the pews on Sunday trying to ignore the images our minds are recalling and to suppress the lustful thoughts of how good the pastor looks in that outfit.

As you sing "Amazing Grace," a voice whispers in your mind, *You should have just stayed home. You are such a hypocrite.* You bow your head to pray, and porn videos start playing as vividly as if you were actually watching them on your phone. You wonder why you even bother. It feels like another level of shame. Is there room for you and your struggle with temptation in the church?

It may even make you question your faith. If you really did love God, then why is this still such a struggle for you? When temptation comes, you may start to pray, read your Bible, or play worship music. Still, you may give in to temptation, and then you wonder if it's all just a joke. Are you just tricking yourself?

The Heart of the Matter

This is perhaps one of my favorite parts of this entire John 4 narrative. For the greater part of this story so far, the Samaritan woman believes she is talking to a stranger who doesn't know anything. He doesn't know her. Doesn't know her past. Doesn't even know the cultural rules and customs. Now, however, Jesus begins to prove her wrong. It turns out he does have an idea of who he is talking to. He reveals he is well aware she doesn't have a husband but has in fact had five and is currently living with a sixth man, whoever he is.

As I mentioned earlier, this particular detail in the story is a point of debate among many scholars. What is meant by "husband"? Had she been married literally to five different men, or had she had five different sexual partners? Was she living with the sixth man or was she involved with a married man? Or do all of these questions not matter because the reference to husbands was figurative?

Whatever he means by it, Jesus reveals that he knows exactly who this woman is. He knows things about her an outsider should not know. He has exposed her.

Her response is to try to guess who Jesus is. She assumes he is a prophet. It's a fair assumption. Jesus has revealed knowledge about her that no strange Jewish man should know. Maybe people in her town would know, but not him.

She could have taken this information and cycled back around to the beginning of their conversation. Why would a Jewish prophet be asking her for water? He of all people definitely should have known better.

But it's almost as if she completely forgets about the water. I think this is because a deeper issue is being explored—a deeper thirst, if you will. She has a question for him, and it is not, "Oh my goodness, how did you know that?" The question is about worship.

"Our ancestors worshiped on this mountain, but you Jews claim that the place where we must worship is in Jerusalem," she says (v. 20).

At first, that may not seem like a big deal, but when you stop to think about it, it is fairly remarkable. Jesus exposes her, and her first response is to ask a question about worship. Is she deflecting? Is she trying to change the subject? Or does this question get even closer to the heart of the issue?

This particular part of their exchange shows us that this isn't just any Samaritan woman. She is, for all intents and purposes, a "religious" woman. She's pointing out that Jews and Samaritans worship in different places. And instead of telling her to stick to the subject, Jesus answers her.

Jesus knows what we fail to remember: worship *is* the subject. It has always been the subject. In any of our struggles with any sin, it is the subject. Your struggle with pornography, lust, masturbation, or fantasy is ultimately about worship. You can take any sin, any struggle, any issue and lay it wide open with the question, "What are you worshiping?"

This is a sobering thought, and I have found it true in my own story. I could say I struggled with pornography for years, but the reality is I didn't "struggle" with it like it was some unwanted pest. I worshiped it. I worshiped sexual release and sexual pleasure all while saying I worshiped Jesus. In my mind, I could somehow compartmentalize the two.

If you haven't caught on to the pattern by now, shame takes healthy desires and thwarts them. We desire to be known and live in community. Shame drives us into isolation. We desire to be loved. Shame calls us unlovable or presents a false love.

Our desire for worship is not unaffected by shame. In fact, it might be what is most affected by shame. Shame presents us with false worship; either we worship false gods or we worship God under false pretenses.

Worshiping False Gods

When asked, "What is worship?" John Piper makes the point that worship starts in the heart. If external activity isn't paired with an inward heart change, then it isn't true worship. He refers to this very passage in John 4 when Jesus responded to the Samaritan woman.

He points out that Jesus paired worship of the spirit with truth, not with the body.

> The inner essence of worship is to know God truly and then respond from the heart to that knowledge by valuing God, treasuring God, prizing God, enjoying God, being satisfied with God above all earthly things. And then that deep, restful, joyful satisfaction in God overflows in demonstrable acts of praise from the lips and demonstrable acts of love in serving others for the sake of Christ.[1]

If you've grown up in a faith culture, you probably have an image of what worship looks like. For me, "worship" meant showing up in my Sunday best, singing the songs, opening the Bible to the right page, and memorizing verses. Worship had a certain look to it. It was an event. We had "worship services" and played music classified as "worship music."

Throughout my entire journey with pornography, I still went to church. Still read my Bible. Still sang the songs. I even performed special music for the congregation. Worship was a program, and I checked all the boxes.

I never considered the idea that I could be worshiping pornography or sexual release through masturbation. No, I worshiped God. I was a Jesus-worshiper who also happened to have a struggle with pornography. Right?

I didn't hold worship services for pornography or write songs glorifying it. But I made space for it. I sang along to songs glorifying sex and promiscuity. I went out of my way, even lied, to be able to carve out time to watch pornography. But because those things happened in private, they seemed less important than what happened in public. In public, I worshiped Jesus.

Meanwhile, in moments of solitude, I worshiped pornography and my own pleasure. It should be no surprise that my heart grew more and more distant from God even as I proclaimed him louder and louder to others.

When we first looked at shame, we saw that one way it can be useful is in pointing out the idols we are worshiping. Perhaps, then, it makes sense that shame seems to show up most in regard to worship, especially when it risks exposing the false gods we've crafted.

Worshiping Ourselves

People will try to say we can have it all. They say we can still love Jesus and do x, y, z, because we've tricked ourselves into believing that x, y, z is a distinct activity from worship. Worship is what we do on Sunday, with raised hands in church. In that way, we tell ourselves we're worshiping God, but when it comes to our time, energy, and resources, it is clear something else has eminence in our lives.

Are you worshiping God, or are you worshiping your own image?

We go to church on Sunday, sing the songs, raise our hands, serve on teams and committees, and call that worship. But we call the time we spend in the darkness, behind closed doors, a struggle. Make no mistake, it is worship, and we are revealing our gods. When we carve out time to search for videos but can't seem to find time to connect with Jesus, we're exposing what we worship.

This is true of so many areas in our lives, not just pornography. Every single sin we struggle with, every single way we fall short of the glory of God, is an attempt to honor, worship, and submit to our own selves.

The self longs to be the idol we worship, and we will daily have a choice to either surrender it or surrender *to* it. I see it in my own heart as a wife and a mother. I worship my alone time and get frustrated when my children interrupt it. I worship my desires and get annoyed when my husband expresses his own needs. We worship ourselves in the name of self-care, rights, and enjoyment.

In Psalm 51, David cries out to God in light of his exposed sin. This took place after he raped Bathsheba and had her husband murdered. When the prophet Nathan confronted David with his sin, David's response was to call out for God to save him from the inside out. He knew it all started with the heart.

David finishes this psalm with this powerful truth that God isn't interested in what we do. He is interested in our hearts: "My sacrifice, O God, is a broken spirit; a broken and contrite heart you, God, will not despise" (v. 17).

Mo Aiken writes,

> God doesn't want your self-reliant promise. . . . He wants your whole heart. . . . But in our self-serving sin we respond, "How about instead of my whole heart I just give you some semi-good behavior?" Then we desperately cling to the hope that, no matter how muddy our heart, that credential looks clean on the surface. And counts for something.[2]

In her book *Stop Calling Me Beautiful*, Phylicia Mason-heimer reflects on John 4 and says of the Samaritan woman,

> Based on her conversation with Jesus, we can infer that she was going through the motions of worship—attending the temple, performing the necessary rites—but she was not in active relationship with God. She did not understand what worship really was—grateful reverence directed toward a personal and loving God.[3]

False Worship of God

Does that mean going to church, reading the Bible, serving, singing, and all of those external representations of worship are wrong? No. Does it mean they are unnecessary? No. But we must remember that the outward expressions of worship are meant to reflect an inner attitude of worship.

This is another way shame can thwart our desire to worship. Instead of worshiping out of a love for God, we worship as a way to "outperform" our struggles. Reading our Bible, praying, serving, and all of those things will not free us from our struggle with pornography, nor will they counterbalance it. We cannot rely on the *actions* of worship to make up for a lack of an *attitude* of worship. In Scripture, we aren't called to put on a show of Bible reading and prayer. Instead, we are told to "put on" or clothe ourselves in Christ (Rom. 13:14 ESV).

Why are you going to church every Sunday? *Why* are you reading your Bible? *Why* do you want to serve? Are you trying to outrun your sin? Are you trying to keep up an image? Are you trying to establish your worth and value and position within a community? Are you trying to prove something to yourself? To God?

We focus on doing all the right things at the right time and acting in the right way simply because we believe God said so. It's robotic and rote obedience, and it doesn't involve our hearts. Such actions are less about worshiping God and more about worshiping our own self-image. We do these things because it makes us feel like we're doing the right thing. We may even truly believe that this checklist is what God wants.

We might believe that if we just do these things long enough then we will finally be free. We try to "fake it until we make it." But that's not the transformation God wants for us. He's not interested in a pile of good behavior trying to crowd out the ways we fail. The works of our faith are important, but they need to be works rooted *in* faith, not fear or shame.

So many of us miss this. We see our friend over there who seems to be growing in her walk with God, so we ask her how she does it. She shares about her Bible study time, her prayer time, and her service on the worship team, so we jump right in copying her. This must be the recipe for success. Instead, it feels like a prison. It feels disingenuous. Have you ever been there? I have.

Why? What causes that? How is it two women with the same struggles can do the same acts of worship and have different "outcomes"?

Because our motives are different, and it's the motivation that makes the difference. If I only go to church because I believe it will help me fight my struggle, or if I only read my Bible because someone told me that's what is going to help me break free from pornography, I'm going to be frustrated with my lack of "progress." Because I haven't done the most important act of worship, and that is surrendering my heart. If my heart is not *in* it, my heart cannot be changed *by* it. Our first act of worship is to change what our heart loves.

The God Who Welcomes Our Worship

But what if your motives are right? What if you want to worship Jesus out of genuine love for him but still find yourself struggling with sin? What if you are the worship leader who leads worship Sunday morning and then falls to pornography on Sunday afternoon?

Place yourself in this story right now as the woman at the well. Jesus has just exposed the thing you have been hiding. He has exposed the skeletons in your closet, and you, in what some might consider an attempt to deflect, ask him about worship. How do you think he would respond?

Some of you already have an answer for that. You imagine it every time you open your Bible or go to church or try to pray. You imagine Jesus saying something like, "Worship?! You're one to talk about worship. You hypocrite. What makes you think I want you to worship me?"

I have heard so many women say things like, "I don't pray anymore because I know God wants nothing to do with me," or "I don't even read my Bible because I can just hear God calling me a hypocrite." Recently a woman shared that she already knows what she is supposed to do, so what's the point of praying? What's the point of asking God for help when she already knows what he is going to say?

This highlights an issue I think many of us have when it comes to church and worship and whether or not Jesus wants us anywhere near him. Contrary to what you may have learned in church, Jesus is ok with sinners worshiping him. In our culture, we have a filtered image of worship. It seems only people with their lives put together are allowed to worship Jesus.

Jesus isn't interested in the worship of self-proclaimed perfect people. He makes this point again and again in the Gospels whenever the first-century self-proclaimed perfect people (otherwise known as Pharisees) try to gatekeep who could worship God.

So this question about whether or not sinners have a "right" to worship Jesus is not new. We find one such example in Luke 7. In this story, Jesus is eating at a Pharisee's house when a woman comes in and anoints his feet. The text tells us that the Pharisee recognizes her as a sinner. He says to himself that if Jesus were a prophet, then he would know what kind of woman was touching him (v. 39).

Now, we don't know what sin this woman struggled with. Some people assume it was sexual sin, but that isn't in the text. All we know is this man classified her as a sinner and took issue with Jesus for allowing her to worship him. He seems to believe that Messiah would *never* let such a woman come close to him.

Does this sound familiar? Have you felt this sort of shame and judgment? From the stage at your church or spoken around the table at your small group, have you ever heard the message that someone "like you" should never be found at the feet of Jesus?

Well, take heart and look at Jesus's response. Even though the text of Luke 7 seems to indicate the Pharisee keeps his thoughts to himself, Jesus still calls him out on it. He then tells a story to prove his point. Two people owed different amounts, one vastly greater than the other. Neither could pay, and both debts were forgiven. Jesus then asks the Pharisee who would love the lender more. The Pharisee guesses it would be the one in greater debt, because a greater debt meant greater forgiveness. Jesus's response is basically, "Bingo."

I hope you see the beauty of this. The depth of your brokenness and depravity doesn't disqualify you from the ability to worship God—and to do so, as John 4 says, "in the Spirit and in truth" (v. 23). That doesn't excuse your need to live righteously, but I hope it gives you a sense of freedom to know that God is not expecting you to clean up your act before you can worship him.

Our struggles and sins do not disqualify us from worship. If you sinned on Saturday night, you can come on Sunday morning to worship. You can realize you are wrong, shut down your internet browser, and practice 1 John 1:9. You confess. He forgives. And then you worship. As scandalous as it may seem, you could sin and watch pornography at 8:00 p.m. on a Saturday, be listening to praise and worship by 8:30 p.m., and show up to church the next morning.

Worship Changes Our Hearts

That can't possibly be right, can it? Does that mean we can just keep watching porn whenever we want as long as we say we're sorry afterward? I mean, if God is going to forgive us, and we can still show up to church, then why not just keep this cycle going? Why not watch porn all week, ask for forgiveness on Sunday morning, and then get to worship in church?

You're not the first person to wonder about the freedom of God's forgiveness. Paul addresses this in Romans 6. The idea was, "Hey! If grace is so great, then why not just keep sinning so we can keep experiencing grace? Sounds like a great plan, right?" Paul very emphatically explains to the Roman church that they were completely missing the point of grace: "What then? Shall we sin because we are not under the law but under grace? By no means!" (v. 15).

Again, we're driving back to motive.

When we keep on sinning because "Hey, there's grace!" we're taking advantage of God's grace and not walking in his love and freedom. If we intentionally spend all week watching porn knowing we can have a "do-over" Sunday morning, it's a safe guess that our worship on Sunday morning isn't genuine. It's also a safe guess that if we are still trying to figure out how to have it both ways, all of the Bible reading and prayer and church attendance in the world will not help us find freedom.

Genuine worship is the avenue for heart change and freedom. Dr. Juli Slattery shares,

People who walk away from porn or give grace to a difficult spouse do so not out of self-discipline but rather because they have experienced a fundamental change in what they love. Spiritual maturity is not primarily what we are able to say no to but the passion and conviction with which we pursue Jesus. Only the Holy Spirit can transform us like this. So, instead of trying to be a good Christian, we learn that our greatest work is to know God, asking Him to overwhelm us with His presence and His power.[4]

I tried to figure out what part of that to highlight for emphasis and I realized I couldn't choose. There is so much power and truth layered in every sentence.

If we are not careful, "worship" becomes a wall between us and God, and legalism is how we attempt to climb it. We legislate how long we need to pray, how often we need to go to church, how many times we need to read through our Bible in a year.

But what happens in the other moments? We can't spend all day every day reading our Bible. We have to interact with people. We encounter stress with work, life, and family. We experience loneliness, boredom, frustration, and fear.

It is in those moments, outside of the church walls, away from our Bible, that our idols are exposed. If my worship of God is a set of rules or something I believe saves me from my sin, then I will be ill-equipped to endure moments of temptation. I'll be frustrated and feel defeated.

But what if I view my interactions with my coworkers and my family as equally as important as my time in church? If I view my response to stress as part of my worship just like my time in prayer, this should change things. Now, instead of worship being a list, it is a lifestyle. In every moment, I can ask myself, *What am I worshiping and why? How can I honor*

God at this moment? It's not about finding a list of rules but finding God's heart for me.

In the previous chapter, I mentioned it will be difficult to love others when we don't understand God's love for us. The same is true of worship. Instead of viewing worship as a list of things we are "supposed" to do as Christians, we need to redefine it as the way we express the love we already have for God. It is not how we earn a seat at God's table; it is what we do with the seat we have been given. When we are assured of God's love for us, we are able to love him in return.

In Romans, when Paul instructs us to "offer our bodies as a living sacrifice" the reason is not "because God said so." Paul points to God's mercy:

> And so, dear brothers and sisters, I plead with you to give your bodies to God *because of all he has done for you.* Let them be a living and holy sacrifice—the kind he will find acceptable. This is truly the way to worship him. (12:1 NLT)

In John 4, when Jesus responded to the woman at the well, he assured her that the way she understood worship was going to change.

> "Woman," Jesus replied, "believe me, a time is coming when you will worship the Father neither on this mountain nor in Jerusalem. You Samaritans worship what you do not know; we worship what we do know, for salvation is from the Jews. Yet a time is coming and has now come when the true worshipers will worship the Father in the Spirit and in truth, for they are the kind of worshipers the Father seeks. God is

spirit, and his worshipers must worship in the Spirit and in truth." (vv. 21–24)

Worship is not about how, when, or how long we read our Bible. Worship is our response to God's love for us. For it to be genuine, we have to believe he loves us and welcomes us to worship him. Authentic worship stems from knowing who it is we are worshiping and how much he loves us. Worship stems from experiencing his love. It is not our way of earning it. And the worshipers who worship God in Spirit and in truth are the worshipers he is seeking.

CHAPTER 7

The Desire for Healing

If you ever need someone to tell you that pornography does a lousy job preparing you for sex, let me be that person. During the years I spent watching pornography, I constantly blamed my struggle with pornography and masturbation on a "high sex drive." I couldn't wait to get married because then I could have sex all the time. That's what I told myself for years: *I am doing this because I have a high sex drive, and when I get married it will all go away.* (For the record, it does not.)

Imagine my surprise when I started planning for my wedding and began panicking about the idea of having sex with my husband. I seriously considered asking to delay the wedding or maybe never getting married at all. At one point, I felt it would be better to be permanently engaged.

Through tears, I reached out to a friend. I shared the chaos in my heart and mind. One sentence in her response made my heart sink: "You need to see somebody." It had been years since I had confessed my struggle with pornography and found freedom. While I still would fall into pornography on rare occasions, for the most part, I felt freed from its grip and its effects.

For years, I had written about how pornography was not representative of sex. I didn't know that from personal experience, of course, but I knew enough about pornography to know it wasn't healthy and wasn't an accurate picture of sex.

So it devastated me to discover this new layer of damage, if you will, just weeks before my wedding. I felt broken and lost. I loved my soon-to-be husband but the idea of having sex with him suddenly terrified me. How did I go from being obsessed with sex while addicted to pornography to being scared of sex weeks before my wedding?

My family had never been a fan of counselors, even though we probably would have benefited greatly from them. Even when divorce and abuse came crashing into our world, we shouldered the burden, never buckling publicly because "Jesus fixes everything." Counselors, we were told, would just keep us stuck or make us look to ourselves or others for excuses. God wanted us to be strong and rely on him. Counselors would give us "worldly answers" and point us away from Jesus. They were ungodly, unbiblical, and likely to lead us astray.

The irony is that I planned to marry one. I decided to try seeing a counselor and set up an appointment with a counselor at our church. I didn't know it at the time, but she was a licensed counselor specializing in trauma.

When the day came, I sat in the parking lot, fearful of dredging up my past with someone who would pry into old, healed wounds. Friends had shared with me that counseling was not a pleasant process. One friend said, "I would feel like my guts were just cut open on the floor, but it was one of the best things I ever did." Not exactly the best way to calm my fears.

I felt convinced my counselor would judge me. She would point out how messed up I was. I feared most of all that she would tell me I shouldn't get married. More than once, I thought of just driving away.

I prayed as I sat in that parking lot, and my prayer started with a heaping dose of asking God what was wrong with me and apologizing for letting him down. Seeing a counselor felt a bit like a failure. I just needed to be stronger.

Even though I had been walking in freedom from pornography for years, shame still had its hooks in me. It took a minute, but I recognized my fear as shame and was able to change my focus. I hadn't signed up for counseling to get over my past but rather I wanted to be able to embrace my future. Failure didn't drive me here; freedom did. Healing did. Hope did.

If Jesus fixes everything, then I went to that counseling session looking for him. While I had spent years following Jesus, loving him, and serving him, it was evident there were still areas of my life I needed him to touch.

At my third counseling session, I brought my fiancé along. During the session, I shared my heartbreak at what I felt I had done to us. I had wounded us with my years-long struggle with pornography. The blame for what we were facing fell squarely on me. I felt so much shame for what I had done.

My counselor leaned in and firmly said, "Stop looking at your past as addiction and sin. That's over. It's forgiven. It's been dealt with. Start looking at it as trauma and abuse." She gave me permission to heal.

In our deepest and darkest moments, what we want more than anything is for God to show up. After experiencing trauma or while dwelling in feelings of hopelessness, we ask where God is, why he didn't intervene. The cry of our hearts is, "God, where are you?" As we wrestle with those questions and find the answers, we find healing.

As a child, when I experienced those moments of pain and trauma, people around me taught me to put up walls between Jesus and the pain. Jesus didn't have time for that brokenness. He didn't have time for my crying. If I really loved him, I wouldn't be hurting because he fixes everything. So much of my woundedness came from believing he wanted nothing to do with the places where I needed him most.

Where Is God?

Every single one of us has had moments like this. No matter how rosy and perfect your life has been, there have been moments when you've wondered what God was thinking. Even now, in your struggle, you've probably cried out wondering why this is so hard. These are the moments you just need God to show up.

This conversation in John 4 ends with the woman expressing what I believe is the ultimate longing of her heart. We've spent verses dancing around this, digging to find it, and here it is. Under all of it—all of the shame, defensiveness, and search for love—is this: a longing for Messiah. Under it all, she is looking for Jesus.

"The woman said, 'I know that Messiah' (called Christ) 'is coming. When he comes, he will explain everything to us.' Then Jesus declared, 'I, the one speaking to you—I am he'" (vv. 25–26).

She is waiting for God to show up. She knows he is coming, and when he comes he is going to explain everything. Jesus could have introduced himself as Messiah from the beginning, but instead, he chooses this moment to reveal who he is. He is Messiah, the Anointed One she has been waiting for.

Sometimes, when we're reading a story, we lose sight of the time it takes for that story to take place. This woman had been waiting for Messiah. She wasn't the only one. The *world* had been waiting for Messiah.

If you've ever read the Gospels (Matthew, Mark, Luke, and John) in order, it might seem like this story takes place later in Jesus's ministry, after he became known for doing miracles. However, it happens near the beginning of his ministry. Any faint whispers of Messiah arriving had likely not reached Samaria. This woman only had hope. She joined the ranks of those like Anna and Simeon, who recognized baby Jesus as the one they had been waiting for.

What a revelation that must have been. When she first met him, he was a strange Jewish man. If he really knew her, he wouldn't be talking to her. But now, she realizes who he is. Not just a man. Not just a Jew. He is *Messiah*. He is the one her heart has been hoping for.

Think for a moment what it would be like to meet someone important. Maybe a record-setting artist, or a record-breaking athlete, or the CEO of a company you hope to work for. You try for weeks, months, maybe even years to gain an audience with this person to no avail. Then, one day, you're at a local coffee shop and a stranger comes up and sits down at your table. They strike up a conversation with you. Eventually, they ask about your hopes and dreams, and, after you share, they reveal that they are, in fact, the person you have been waiting for. That would likely go down as one of your "best days ever!"

That must be how it was for this woman. *Messiah* made time to be with her. Jesus very well could have joined the disciples on their excursion to get food. He could have gone into town with them and announced himself there. Instead, he stood there, with her. One-on-one.

The good news is, that's exactly how it is *for us*.

God Is Near

Some of us fear this kind of encounter with God. We fear that at the end of repentance is more judgment. We crave that relationship and yet cower at the thought of it. When we ask the question, "God, where are you?" we think his response will be, "Why on earth do you think I want to deal with you?"

As it is with our desire for relationships with people, the nearness of God is something we yearn for while simultaneously fearing it could be the end of us.

In Psalm 73:28, the psalmist says, "But as for me, God's presence is my good. I have made the Lord GOD my refuge, so I can tell about all you do" (CSB). Some versions translate "presence" as "nearness." The psalmist declares that God's nearness is good, but you might feel just the opposite. You may feel God's nearness is bad news.

While many of us long to feel safe and find refuge in God, I think the truth is we can't because we're too afraid of God's judgment. Our hearts and minds feel fragile and weary from the battle they have waged for years. Though we feel broken by it, we also feel somewhat responsible, and the fear is that when we ask for help, instead of finding it, we'll find we are truly on our own.

You may have even experienced this when you shared your story with a friend or when your partner found out about your struggle. The nearness and closeness of those relationships plus the knowledge of something so intimate may have had devastating consequences. Your parents may have refused to talk about it. Your best friend may have ghosted you. Your husband may have refused to be intimate with you.

It can feel like you're going to break under the weight of all of this. You fiercely guard hope because it feels like your life might very well depend on it. It's as if all of your broken pieces are being held together so delicately. One wrong move could send them crashing down in a wounded and wounding mess. The response from everyone around you sounds like, "Well, if you don't want to do this anymore, just stop. Why are you telling me about it?" Others often don't realize how vulnerable, broken, and beyond help we can feel in the moments our brokenness is revealed.

In Christian cultures, we've often emphasized the need for repentance and even confession while completely ignoring the very real need for hope and healing. Confession says, "This is where I am." Repentance says, "I want to get out." Hope asks, "Can I get out?" And healing asks, "How can I get out?"

For many of us, it is our brokenness that is keeping us stuck.

Healing and Freedom

My journey of freedom began with confession in Bible college. This was the year after I was told women didn't have pornography problems. The year after I sent nudes to a complete stranger. The year after this high school valedictorian dropped out of college so she could be a porn star.

It probably wouldn't surprise you if I told you I struggled a bit at Bible college. I didn't have access to pornography because of filters on the school's internet, but you don't need access to indulge. Pornography is unique like that.

So, even in Bible college, where every class was on the Bible or about the Bible, where we had scheduled time for Bible reading, where we had nightly devotions as a group and prayer . . . I still struggled. I was frustrated because it felt like I wasn't growing, like my prayers were bouncing off the ceiling. Where was God, and why wasn't he answering me?

Partway through my first semester, the dean staff held an all-women's meeting. There they taught on strongholds from 2 Corinthians 10. They shared that a stronghold was an area of our lives where the devil still had a foothold. From the stage, they said, "We know some of you struggle with pornography and masturbation, and we are here to help." Then they encouraged us to share our strongholds, whatever they were.

After years of wearing a mask, I finally ripped it off with a simple sentence written on paper: "My name is Jessica Harris and my stronghold is pornography."

I thought that would be enough for me to be free. I thought this confession would automatically lead to freedom and expected to feel a weight lifted. Instead, I felt even more scared, threatened, and trapped.

I instantly regretted my decision to share. I felt angry. It wasn't fair that this was my struggle. I knew the girl next to me probably wrote down something cute like, "My name is Christian Barbie and my stronghold is I don't read my Bible for thirty minutes a day."

Why couldn't I have a "cute" stronghold?

My anger quickly morphed to fear and shame. As I walked back to my dorm room, terror and desperation filled my heart. Shame screamed loud in my ears. *What have you done? They lied to you. They don't want to help you. They're just going to send you home. You can never be free. You're too messed up.*

In one of the most desperate prayers I have ever prayed, I begged God for that voice to be wrong. "God, this has to work. I've tried everything. I know how far I can fall. I know where the last 'confession' took me. If they lied to me and they can't help me, I don't know what else to do."

I couldn't see a way out right then. Confession did not feel good. It seemed harsh and blinding. I felt weak and vulnerable. I held on desperately to the possibility that freedom was somehow on the other side of this. I couldn't see it and I certainly couldn't feel it, but I clung to the hope that there was life and a way out somewhere.

Healing and Hope

Hope is a fragile thing at times. We long for it and are afraid of losing it. We want to believe God is good and that his nearness to us and knowledge of us are good. At the same time, we believe God to be some sort of spiteful, vengeful, hate-filled judge ready to lash out at us. But this, again, is shame.

Is God holy? Yes.[1] Does he require justice? Yes.[2] Is he sick and tired of you sinning and ready to strike you down the next time you fall? No.[3] If you come to him and ask for his help, will he tell you to figure it out yourself? No.[4]

The Bible college staff had promised to help, and they did. I credit the effectiveness of their help in part to their focus on healing. One staff member served as my accountability partner. The others involved in my journey seemed to be more concerned with answering the question, Who is Jessica without pornography? My journey of freedom ran like train tracks parallel to my journey of healing.

Pornography, lust, fantasy, and masturbation had become second nature to me. All roads led to them. Any emotion—good or bad—led to them. Any free time led there. It turns out a high sex drive didn't motivate my time in pornography as much as my desire to escape and cope with life did.

Trying to stop cold turkey without addressing the depth of my brokenness and the healing I needed would have left me weak, struggling, and likely failing. Their focus on healing and inviting God into those broken places helped me find true freedom. They helped me tear down the walls I'd built between God and my pain and realize God does care if I'm hurting. They introduced me to the *tenderness* of God.

The Broken Road to Your Struggle

Our takeaway from John 4 is Jesus is the living water, but there is depth to that statement beyond salvation and eternal life. When that living water spills into our deepest longings, we experience healing for our brokenness.

Healing isn't something we often discuss when it comes to sexual struggles. We take our brokenness to be a punishment for what we've done wrong. If you're single, you may wonder if your singleness is God's way of making you pay. The same holds true if your marriage is struggling, if you have experienced loss, or if you are struggling with things like infertility.

Sadly, some of us may have even grown up in families where this sort of punishment occurred often. Phrases like, "You've made your bed. Now you have to lie in it," or "Well, you should have thought about that before you chose to do such and such" are all too familiar. We have learned a sort of long-range punishment for our choices. Natural consequences are one thing, but sometimes it has been taken to the next level. We're told we have one shot to get it right, and when we get it wrong, we're a failure, a screwup. Instead of experiencing consequences for our actions, we experience a lingering shame for our choices.

Past wrongs are held over us, weaponized, and used to invalidate our pain and struggle. Because this is the model we've seen in real life, it's hard for us to believe God operates differently. This is a toxic mindset to apply to any sin we struggle with but especially pornography. With its ease of access and addictive nature, pornography feels like something we can never escape. It is the thing we can never not choose. Even without technology, our brains can house hours of videos and images, ready for us to indulge whenever and wherever we want to.

Pornography is unique in two ways. First, it is the only struggle we can become. We cannot become alcohol, drugs, or even video games, but we can become pornography. I found that out at age seventeen when I sent nudes to a stranger. I turned my body over to him to use however he chose, getting satisfaction without any sort of relationship. Fundamental damage occurred that day. I, a person, became a thing.

The other thing unique about pornography is we can never cut off access. Ever. Our brains are amazing and powerful supercomputers capable of storing hundreds if not thousands of images and videos, ready to be accessed. We may be days, even weeks, without the technology to view pornography and still struggle. I can attest we can even be years removed from pornography and still have images recalled at the most inopportune times.

What does this mean for those of us who struggle? Does it mean finding freedom is impossible? Are we destined for hopeless lives haunted by images we no longer wish to recall?

No. What it means is that simply not watching pornography anymore is not enough. So often programs and pursuits are centered on that goal: "get me to stop watching pornography." We install content blockers and accountability filters, blacklist websites, and burn romance novels, all in an effort to eradicate pornography from our lives. But we can't, because our brains still store it. This is why freedom focused solely on eradicating pornography will not be effective.

Instead, our focus should be on healing the roads leading us to pornography. We cannot cut off access no matter how hard we try, but we can cut off necessity. What are the deeper roots driving us to this place? What are the wounds branching out of this struggle? If we fail to address the brokenness and only focus on stopping pornography, we may be tempted to sub in other methods of self-comfort like disordered eating, alcoholism, drugs, and self-harm.[5]

The Broken Road from Your Struggle

Even if you would say no brokenness led you to pornography, pornography itself can do damage.

Staci Sprout discovered pornography before the age of the internet when she found a *Playboy* stashed in her dad's sock drawer. Now she is a licensed therapist who specializes in helping people recover from sex, love, and relationship addiction. She points out that pornography can wound girls and women in many ways. These wounds encompass everything from how a woman views herself to how she functions in relationships. For example, consumption of pornography can cause a woman to develop "chronic hateful self-objectification," to create unrealistic expectations and misunderstandings about sex, to associate sex with violence, and to damage her sexual functioning.[6]

Over the years, the church has made the mistake of ignoring such damage or accepting it as a consequence of our actions. Is it so radical to believe God would want to heal that? The nature of the gospel and grace demands that when we talk about freedom from sin, we also talk about healing from its effects.

You have ended up where you are through a series of choices on your part and the part of others. Your quest to escape that brokenness has led you here, and your brokenness will try to keep you here. It's a vicious cycle, one we often overlook in our preoccupation with trying to stop unwanted behavior.

The God Who Heals

The pursuit of God's heart necessitates a pursuit of healing. If I believe God is good and he is able, and that Jesus came for the "sick," then I have to believe he desires to heal the broken areas of my life. If I believe Jesus came to rescue and restore, then I have to believe that his rescue and restoration extend into areas of woundedness. If I believe he loves me, then I have to believe he cares for me and cares about my healing.

That healing does not happen through ignorance. It happens through inviting God into those places of brokenness. Sometimes it happens with outside help. If you broke your leg, I hope you would seek appropriate medical care. Yes, you may temporarily splint it so it doesn't get worse, but you wouldn't just get up the next day and start walking on it. We understand getting help when it comes to our physical bodies, but we tend to take a more isolated approach when it comes to sin issues.

What if I told you your body is at play in this struggle too?

No, the damage isn't as obvious as a broken leg, but over time pornography use has been changing your brain, rewiring it, teaching it, and training it to want, crave, seek out, and protect pornography.[7] Yes, we may be able to "splint" our brains with password protection and accountability software, but if we don't pursue a more holistic approach to healing and freedom, we will find ourselves continually returning to this place.

If all we focus on is stopping the behavior and breaking free from the addiction, we're only getting part of what God wants for us. When we view ourselves as deserving of punishment, we rob ourselves of the opportunity to experience the healing God offers. We simply can't live a life serving God if we're convinced he's out to get us.

We are lying to ourselves if we believe all God cares about is whether or not we are acting the way we are supposed to. We are lying to ourselves about God if we believe that actions matter more than the deeper, wounded places of our hearts. God is a healer. He is a redeemer. He is a renewer and a restorer.

In John 10, we read an account of Jesus conversing with Pharisees. Jesus likens believers to sheep and calls himself the Good Shepherd. Nestled in this passage is the declaration that Jesus came to give life, and life abundantly. This is in contrast to the thief who comes to steal, kill, and destroy (vv. 10–11). If Jesus is offering abundant life in contrast to the death brought by the "thief," we can conclude that Jesus offers to return what was stolen, revive what has died, and rebuild what has been destroyed.

If our reliance on God begins and ends with just getting out of pornography, we're missing out on the abundance he offers each of us. It isn't "looking for excuses" to pursue healing, to walk broken paths hand in hand with our redeemer. It isn't an abundant life if we're living busted up, limping, and wounded—and we aren't fooling anybody by just trying harder. Finding freedom from a struggle is pointless if we don't also find healing.

CHAPTER 8

A Long Walk Redeemed

Deciding to share my story was not easy. After a lot of heart work in college, I felt like I was finally walking in freedom. I could say no to my desires for pornography and fantasy. That didn't mean I never turned back to them again, but I had severed the control they had over me. I had let God into the dark places to do his healing work. Then, I figured, it was time for me to move on with my life.

When I'd graduated from high school, I'd planned on being a doctor. My stint in Bible college was an unexpected but great detour, and the time had come to get back on track. I tucked my struggle with pornography away in a box and stored it in the attic of my heart, content to never talk about it again.

We see how that went. How, then, did I end up here?

Well, I kept applying to schools, getting accepted, but then having zero peace about moving forward. I tried changing majors, changing schools, anything to find the right combination that brought peace. When I stopped and prayed about what God wanted me to do, the answer was *share your story.*

I told him no and took off in the opposite direction, like Jonah on the ship to Tarshish. My prayer years earlier had been, "God, I'll do anything for you, but pornography comes with me." That had changed to, "God, I'll do anything for you, but my past in pornography *cannot* come with me." I had zero interest in sharing this part of my life. It was the last thing I wanted anyone to know about me.

For two years, I refused to share my story. When I finally made my website, I did it out of anger. It felt like some sort of penance and a deal with God. No doors were opening up anywhere. No schools. No mission boards. No marriage prospects. I felt like God was refusing to bless me until I did this, like a parent refusing to give their child dessert until they finish all their broccoli. So I sulked and bitterly created a website. *What kind of opportunistic, mean God would make me do something like this?*

I tried to keep it anonymous. I believe I first called my blog "Purity After Pornography." Simple, straight, to the point. Within months, I had speaking requests and a choice. You can write anonymously, but it's not easy to be an anonymous speaker. If I wanted to step into this calling, I was going to have to be known.

That was over ten years ago now. I've traveled the world and sat across from women who felt they were alone in this struggle. I've had the opportunity to share my story not because it is glamorous and fun—it is not—but because it's how I met Jesus. And I've learned so much about the depths of God's grace and this beautiful promise we have of redemption. Grace redeems our stories.

At this point in the John 4 narrative, the woman leaves her water jug by the well and heads back to town to tell everyone she's met Jesus. Her testimony isn't, "Hey, there's this guy at the well who says he is Messiah" but rather, "Come, see a man who told me everything I ever did. Could this be the Messiah?" (v. 29).

Her testimony is born out of the conversation she had with Jesus at the well, a conversation *he* initiated and sustained. This whole story would have had a different feel if she had come to the well and he had just said, "Hi, I'm Messiah." Instead, he spent time with her. This conversation is the longest one-on-one conversation captured in the Gospels.[1] Her testimony isn't simply that Jesus met her but that Messiah knows her and has revealed himself to her.

In response to her testimony, the people of the town come out to see Jesus. Later in the chapter, we see that many of the townspeople believe because of her testimony (v. 39). They invite Jesus to stay with them. He stays for two days, and even more of the townspeople come to believe him because of his own teaching.

This woman's encounter with Jesus led an entire town to him. She walked to the well alone, unknown. After encountering Messiah, she walked that road again, leading a town to him. If that path had been marked by shame and isolation before, now that memory was rewritten. This path no longer cemented her identity in shame; it cemented her identity in Jesus.

Our Mistaken Identity

Understanding our identity is part of understanding God's heart for us. If my husband says I'm beautiful, I have a choice. I can either trust him and believe what he says he sees in me, or I can blow off his comment and mutter to myself about all the ways he is mistaken. Which response is rooted and grounded in trust and love? Which response is rooted in our relationship?

The Bible is filled with verses that support the truth and reality of God's love and his compassion toward us. One beautiful example is the story of the prodigal son, told in Luke 15:11–32. A selfish, impulsive son demands his part of the inheritance from his father. Then he runs off and has a great time living the high life for a while. Eventually, the money runs out, and the fun leaves along with it. He finds himself alone, working with pigs (which would have been repulsive to the Pharisees hearing this story). The Bible says the prodigal comes to his senses and heads for home.

Every single thing that happened to him came as a result of his own choices. He *chose* to take his inheritance. He *chose* to spend it on having a good time. No one made him do that. He made those choices. They landed him in a muddy field eyeing pig food with longing, and in that depth, he made another choice. He chose to make his way home.

The father could have locked the door and never let him in, or allowed him to return but made him work to earn back his inheritance. He could have let him in but never let him live down his choices. This is what the son expected. He didn't expect to waltz back home and right back into sonship. He was willing to settle for being a servant if it meant a roof over his head and food in his belly.

And that's exactly where you might be. You might be knee-deep in mud, isolated by shame, and so starved of relationship that you're considering doing things you would have never dreamed of doing in a million years. Desperate, you turn your heart toward home, figuring God will let you sleep in some dirty back room. You imagine yourself like Cinderella, locked away from the world, dressed in rags, eating scraps, and scrubbing the floors. You, like the prodigal, assume that's your place in God's house.

But the prodigal son found a different reception, and so will you.

Instead of encountering a scornful, vengeful father, the prodigal encountered love—passionate love. Love that would run up to a son covered in mud and reeking of pig manure and embrace him. Love that would call for the best robe, sandals, and a ring. Love that would, instead of putting that lousy, undeserving son to work, throw a party celebrating his homecoming.

You are that son, and you may be rehearsing the encounter in your head. *God, I am so sorry. I know I really screwed up. I don't deserve to be called your child.* You think he's going to say, "Yeah, you screwed up. Here are your rags. Get to work." But that's not grace.

This is the power of the message of grace. It would be enough if God just reached down and unlocked the chains that bound us. It would be enough if he handed us a rag to clean up and gave us a little shelter from the storm. But he wants to do more. Grace is about rescue and restoration. We're clothed in Christ (Gal. 3:27). We're raised to walk in newness of life with him (Rom. 6:8–14). We are made new.

In 2 Corinthians 5:17, we read "Therefore, if anyone is in Christ, he is a new creation. The old has passed away; behold, the new has come" (ESV).

We have to stop viewing ourselves as just "converted sinners," as if sin still has some claim to our story. My friends in *Free to Thrive* say, "We don't call butterflies converted caterpillars."[2] We call them by a new name, recognizing they are completely different creatures.

We can make the mistake of trying to walk a redemption story that is obsessed with all we've ever done wrong. We find our identity primarily in our struggle. We are porn addicts, lustful women in need of a Savior. Unworthy. Like lepers outside the camp, we cry out "Unclean!"

But what if we were to shift our perspective?

We aren't rotten, terrible people who "just so happen" to be loved by God, like that's some accessory to our primary identity. We are first and foremost daughters of the Most High King. If you believe the good news of Jesus's sacrifice on your behalf, it's not meant to make you feel guilty. Don't walk around telling yourself, *I'm a terrible person. Look what I made God have to do.*

When we make that shift and realize that our primary identity isn't in our struggle but in our Savior, it changes us. I can believe God desires me because he has told me as much. He has proven it.

As a wife, I have a choice. I can live every moment of every day reminding my husband what a wreck of a person I am and question why he loves me. Or I can rest in his love and let my identity shift. It doesn't matter what I think of me. What matters in our relationship is that he has chosen me.

We have chosen each other. Could he have chosen someone else? Sure. But he didn't.

We are chosen.

When shame starts to make you question why God loves you or second-guess that he could even desire you, respond with who you are. Your identity in Christ. You are a daughter he loves dearly, not some stray he cannot stand.

The Labels Others Give

Sometimes the issue isn't believing God can redeem our stories as much as convincing *others* to believe he can. The woman at the well walked back into her village and shared about Jesus openly, which causes some readers to question whether or not she was shunned to begin with. For us, though, encounters with shame in the church can be all too real. Grace is scandalous, and some people take issue with the idea that God can redeem and use people with so-called checkered pasts.

Even while writing this book, I have had to navigate relationships with people who discovered my past. I do not walk around in my everyday life introducing myself as "Jessica Harris who writes about pornography." Discernment is not the same as duplicity, and I am careful not to introduce that information into a situation in which it is not appropriate. Sometimes, however, I share it so people will hear it from me first, as was the case recently when I volunteered to serve on a women's ministry team. I chose to reveal that I speak and write on this topic not because the topic was important but because I wanted the team to know I was a speaker and a writer.

Their response was unexpected and painful. After weeks of complete silence, some of the older women requested a special meeting to discuss "the porn issue." They were skeptical about whether or not I was truly free. Could people *be* free from pornography? They didn't want the poison of pornography to "infect" the entire ministry. This kind of response may sound noble, but in reality it's just shame masquerading as wisdom.

The prodigal son has a brother, and this brother is not at all thrilled about the prodigal's antics. When the father receives the wayward son back into the family, the faithful son complains. He mopes about in the field and refuses to celebrate his brother's return.

Friend, you are going to run into your fair share of angsty brothers.

We all love a good survivor story. We praise determination, hope, and miracles. But a sinner story is less inspiring. We feel the sinner should have known better, so they don't deserve a platform. But the story has never been about the survivor or the sinner. The story has always been about God, and God is the rescuer either way. He is the redeemer either way. He's more than capable of taking those pieces that are broken and making them right, showcasing his grace, glory, and redemptive power in our lives.

God saving us from our sinful selves, setting us free, and transforming us into his image isn't a lesser grace. The Samaritan woman's testimony was "He told me all I ever did," and it was *that* testimony that brought a town to Jesus.

The Reason Things Happen

That doesn't mean God ordains our struggles. Please don't take all of this as an excuse to stay in pornography. Do not tell yourself, *Well, great! If God can redeem this, then let me sink even lower so I have a stronger testimony.* That isn't how this works.

I think Romans 8:28 may be one of the most grossly misused verses in all of Scripture: "And we know that in all things God works for the good of those who love him, who have been called according to his purpose." We twist this verse, pull it, and stretch it to mean things like, "Everything happens for a good reason."

God does not ordain evil. That day your uncle molested you, God wasn't callously sitting in heaven saying, "It's ok; everything happens for a reason." When you log on to that website, God isn't saying, "That's ok; I can make something good out of this." Everything does happen for a reason. Sometimes, that reason is sin.

We make a grave mistake if we assume everything in life happens because God wants it to happen that way. We begin to cast God as some puppet master guilty of crimes by proxy. When you accuse God of being responsible for all of the hurt and pain ever dealt to you and every sin you've struggled with, assuming they're some part of his master plan, then it's no wonder you have a hard time viewing him as a loving, caring Creator. Rather he's an evil mastermind, forcing you to struggle to promote his agenda.

It makes no sense and flies in the face of God's character.

Sin, hurt, and pain all grieve his heart. If you want an illustration, look no further than John 11:35. Jesus wept over Lazarus's death even though he knew he was going to raise Lazarus from the dead. He did not look at Lazarus's sisters and tell them to stop crying. He cried with them.

We live in a broken world filled with imperfect people exercising their free will, often to the detriment and injury of others. Sometimes we do it to ourselves.

Have you ever looked at a broken and wounded area of your life and wondered what, exactly, God's plan was for it? Maybe you've stepped back and surveyed the wreckage of an area of your life and thought, *Nothing good can come out of this.*

That may be how you feel about your struggle with pornography. It just seems like a giant splotch on your life, and there is no way God can do anything with it. You may even blame him for it. After all, if he would just take away your sex drive, break your phone, or *do something*, then it wouldn't be a problem anymore.

God did not ordain it, but that doesn't mean he can't *redeem* it.

Understanding that changes how you fight, because, let's be honest, if you think God "ordained" your struggle with pornography, you will never experience freedom. If you think he is somehow doing this to you, that he is keeping you stuck and it's ok because "everything happens for a reason," you're wrong. You will be waiting around, blaming God for not saving you from a struggle he started. When he doesn't smash your phone for you, you'll shrug your shoulders and say, "Well, I guess it is his will."

No. It is not.

This can be a problem for us when we start to value the reason over the redemption. We become more focused on why we're here than how on earth we get out. We may feel there is no way out, so we try to make sense of it by blaming God for it.

If you believe, instead, that sin—namely yours—got you into this mess and God can redeem your story, that changes things. It gives you hope. God doesn't force us to sin; James 1:13 tells us he can't. It's against his nature to lead us into sin. But since the beginning of time, he has always had a plan to rescue us, redeem us, and restore us to a relationship with him. He can take our long walks to the well and redeem them, turning them into something that brings him glory.

An Incomplete Redemption

I wish I had the space to share all the ways I've seen this play out in my life over the years. Not long after I started speaking, I led a ladies' workshop at a conference in Canada. Word spread that I would be veering from standard Christian beauty, modesty, and dating messages and speaking on lust. By the time my session began, every chair in the room was full, and women were standing around the edges of the room and sitting on the floor up front.

God did amazing work in that room. I watched women share deep struggles. I watched strongholds fall. As I left, I thought, *They didn't come for me. No one knows who I am. They came for Jesus.* I realized I had a choice. If I knew women were trapped and struggling and I also knew a way out, how could I leave them there? How could I not lead them to Jesus? And the best way I had to do that was through my own story.

Several years later, I decided to put my story on paper. I'd hesitated because I truly believed publishing my story would be a death sentence for my hopes and dreams of marriage. No man in his right mind would ever want to be associated with me—a woman who writes and speaks on her own past with pornography. The only reason I wrote my first book, *Beggar's Daughter*, when I did was because I was dating a man who supported it. We broke up just before I finished the book. I completed it, and for the next year felt a bit like my life was over. I struggled with feeling that God was just exploiting my hurt for his entertainment.

My life, even in freedom, had somehow been defined by my past struggle with pornography. It was the hinge point of my identity. My writing centered on it, and I had begun to identify myself primarily as a former addict. Any time I experienced negative emotions or circumstances, I blamed it on my past with pornography.

That's not how you live if you truly believe in grace. That's how life looks when you try to juggle freedom and shame. Free, but only sort of. Healed, but still damaged.

In that year, when I was at my deepest and lowest, humiliated that my story was out there for the world to see, a chaplain ordered my book. As I felt like nothing good could come from all of this mess, that chaplain read my story. Just when I was ready to pack everything up and retreat to where I would feel safe and life would be "easy," he sent me an email. He wanted a case of the book—and a chance to get to know me better. I said yes to the first request and tried to ignore the second.

To hear our best friends tell the story, his friend was cheering him on while I was asking my friend how to get this pesky pastor to go away. We got married a year after that initial email.

I thought publishing my story in a book would be the end of every other hope and dream I had in my life. It felt like burning a bridge; I would walk around permanently shamed and wounded and scarred. It is not lost on me that sharing my story is the very thing that welcomed a new level of the riches of grace in my life.

In our first few months of marriage, I often blamed my past for our difficulties. Any breakdown in communication or clumsiness surrounding sex I just knew was somehow my fault, and it would grieve me. My husband, in all of his grace and love and wisdom, spoke truths to the lies he knew were trying to grab hold of my heart. More than once he wrapped me in his arms and said, "You are whole. You are healed. You are redeemed. You are loved."

The God Who Redeems

I want you to picture your story as it is right now, with all of its struggle, sin, brokenness, and evil. Shame owns your story right now. Darkness wields that shame over you with power. It threatens you with it. Your story is essentially held ransom by your struggle and sin. *Oh, you want to be known? Are you sure about that? You realize that if they know you, then they are going to know this? And then no one is going to love you.* It's blackmail. Do you feel held hostage by your story, even as you consider freedom?

In Ephesians 1:7–8, Paul writes, "In him we have redemption through his blood, the forgiveness of sins, in accordance with the riches of God's grace that he lavished on us."

That word translated "redemption" means to pay a ransom. Sin holds your story hostage. Shame hangs it over your head. But grace comes in and buys it back. God pays the ransom. You don't earn it. You don't work your way out of it.

When you are stuck in the depths of your story, in the moments and memories tattered by pain and brokenness, where sin's teeth and evil's claws have sunk in and punctured your heart, Jesus, in his love, grace, and desire for you, steps up and says, "Let her go. That story now belongs to me." He redeems us. He buys back our stories.

Sit with that for a while. It brings tears to my eyes just writing it.

This is the beauty of redemption.

Guess what, friend. If pornography is part of your story, there is no unwriting that. Jesus steps into it. Sometimes we try to share G-rated versions of our stories in an effort to distance ourselves from the shame of our struggle, but God wants to and can redeem every part of our stories.

The power of our stories isn't that we love our wounds but that there is a God who loves us in our woundedness and redeems it. There is a God who looks at us in our sin and brokenness and says, "That one, right there. She's mine. Just watch what I can do with her."

God can use your story to bring others to himself, though it may not be in the pages of a book or in words spoken from a stage. His story of grace in your life can point others to his grace. Our long walks, the areas of our lives that threatened to swallow us in shame, can be redeemed. Those broken paths can now lead us, and others, to Jesus.

CHAPTER 9

A Desire Satisfied

At the beginning of this book, I asked if you believed God desires you. Even as you've read through these chapters, you might have felt like God desires something from you more than he desires you. I think many of us struggle with that. We see nothing in ourselves worth desiring.

Perhaps you've been taught that God is always somewhat annoyed with you. He's been presented as a cosmic frustrated parent or some sort of divine first responder. These distorted views of God can cause us to live life feeling like an inconvenience. We can't have a right relationship with God if we don't view our relationship with him rightly.

I've been blessed to share the stage with Josh McDowell and Ben Bennett at "porn conferences" around the world, and this is something we have seen in our ministry. As they share in *Free to Thrive,*

As we've traveled the world meeting people and ministering to them, we've found that many have the wrong God—they don't see him for who he truly is. They harbor wrong assumptions and core beliefs about his character. They see him as (or suspect him to be) angry, obsessed with rules, and distant.

These views about God are toxic to our wellbeing and prevent us from thriving in life. Fulfillment in life comes from knowing our Creator, experiencing his love for us, and understanding his intention for us to flourish.[1]

Do you feel like you annoy God?

As I struggled with pornography, lust, and fantasy, as a teen I would hear things like, "Every time you sin, you are nailing Christ to the cross again." It was a heartbreaking mental picture. The guilt provoked was, at times, overwhelming. I imagined God getting frustrated with me. Many days I would wake up, determined that yesterday was the last day I would struggle. That was it. God needed me to stop. Jesus needed me to stop. I was hurting him. Hurting his heart.

Then it felt like my feet were on autopilot as I'd walk into my mom's bedroom and take my place in front of the computer. Hours of pornography later, I would be overcome with guilt and frustration.

What is wrong with me? Why can't I break this?

I was sure I was disappointing God, and, for years, adopted the phrase "frustrating grace." I thought it was biblical. After all, it's right there in Galatians 2:21, where Paul says "I do not frustrate the grace of God" (KJV). I started to live in this cycle of believing that there was a certain number of times a day I could mess up before God would be frustrated with me. Yet I also knew his mercies are new every morning (Lam.

3:22–23). After I'd hit my daily "limit," I would just wait until the next morning, because then I knew God and I were "starting over."

If you read Galatians 2:21 in context, you'll see when Paul talks about frustrating grace, he means something quite different. I grew up in a church that used the King James Version, so this was the only way I had ever read this verse: "I do not frustrate the grace of God: for if righteousness come by the law, then Christ is dead in vain" (KJV).

In other versions, the intent is clearer. The ESV reads, "I do not nullify the grace of God, for if righteousness were through the law, then Christ died for no purpose." And the NIV reads, "I do not set aside the grace of God, for if righteousness could be gained through the law, Christ died for nothing!"

"Frustrating grace" is not about getting on God's nerves because we keep sinning. Grace doesn't expect us to attain our own righteousness. Trying to attain it ourselves is exactly how grace is frustrated. Our failures don't frustrate grace. Believing we have to do this *without* grace does. Christ died because we're never going to be able to get our act together. The message of grace is that we need grace.

If we're going through life essentially telling God, "No, no! I got this. I can do this. I don't need your help. Thanks for the offer, though," *that* is what frustrates, sets aside, or nullifies grace.

Looking at the Harvest

I want to invite you into a part of this John 4 story that we almost always overlook. The woman leaves her water jug and runs back to town (v. 28). We call her one of the first missionaries, which ties in nicely when we print verse 35 on flyers to promote our missions conferences: "Don't you have a saying, 'It's still four months until harvest'? I tell you, open your eyes and look at the fields! They are ripe for harvest."

I'd heard about the fields being ripe for harvest many times in church. It is the motivational altar call verse for evangelization. I didn't realize it comes smack in the middle of this story. It is part of a conversation between Jesus and the disciples that I have never, in all of my years attending church, heard preached in its context. But I think there is power in keeping the story together.

The disciples had left Jesus at the well so they could go into town to grab food (v. 8). They come back with that food near the end of Jesus's conversation with the woman, just after Jesus indicates he is Messiah. When they show up on the scene, they say nothing about Jesus speaking with the woman (v. 27).

Remember how the woman responded to Jesus's request for water? She was a bit shocked because he was breaking all of the rules. The disciples would have been aware of these same cultural standards, so this would have been a scandal for them too.

He was still a Jewish man talking to a Samaritan woman at a well, and the text seems to indicate that they could have questioned it. They could have asked her what she wanted or asked Jesus why he was talking to her, but they didn't. Instead, it seems they stand by, watching, just waiting until she leaves.

Once the woman heads for town, the disciples offer Jesus food. Jesus tells the disciples he is no longer hungry.

Meanwhile his disciples urged him, "Rabbi, eat something."

But he said to them, "I have food to eat that you know nothing about."

Then his disciples said to each other, "Could someone have brought him food?"

"My food," said Jesus, "is to do the will of him who sent me and to finish his work." (vv. 31–34)

The disciples are confused. Again, Jesus is using a physical picture to illustrate a spiritual truth.

It's as if the story starts playing over from the beginning, just with different characters. The woman had come to the well for physical water, and Jesus offered her water to quench her spiritual thirst. Now the disciples come to the well offering Jesus physical food, and he reveals spiritual food. The water he'd offered the woman led to everlasting life. The food he speaks of now is "to do the will of him who sent me and to finish his work."

What changed for the woman who came to the well? She met Jesus.

What changed for *Jesus*? He met her.

But she didn't have anything to offer him. In fact, from what we can tell, she never even gave him the drink he originally requested. Jesus has gained nothing from her during this interaction, and yet he is satisfied.

He tells the disciples it is because he is doing God's will and finishing God's work. What is that work?

Restoring a Relationship

What did Jesus offer the woman at the well? Himself? Sure. But beyond that, reconciliation. He knew all she ever did, knew exactly what she had done, and still offered himself. This woman stood face-to-face with the long-awaited Messiah and didn't face judgment or shame but instead encountered patience and grace.

And this interaction didn't burden Jesus. It didn't suck the life out of him.

I'm an introvert. Any interaction with a stranger in a strange situation that requires something of me inevitably leaves me feeling drained. But this interaction between Jesus and the Samaritan woman left both feeling satisfied. She because she had met Messiah, and he because he had done the will of God and "finished the work."

In other words, Jesus walked away from this encounter satisfied because this is what he came to do. Paul emphasizes this in 2 Corinthians 5:19, writing that "in Christ God was reconciling the world to himself, not counting their trespasses against them" (ESV).

God's heart is not punishment. It is reconciliation.

What does that mean?

The primary definition and usage for *reconcile* has to do with restoring to relationship. Have you ever fought with a close friend or a family member? Maybe you said something you shouldn't have, or they said something hurtful, and it left both of you wounded and distant. You may have blocked each other on social media or maybe cut off the friendship altogether. A friend and I once had a very heated argument that ended with her kicking me out of her wedding and us not talking for nearly a year. We eventually talked it through and are still great friends to this day.

Sometimes my husband and I will have a misunderstanding that leaves one or both of us frustrated and hurt. My usual response is to begin cleaning our house, closing cupboard doors a little louder than necessary just to express my annoyance. His usual response is to sit quietly on the couch and pray and wait for me to run out of things to scrub and fold before I plop down on the couch beside him. No matter how frustrating the disconnect, we have promised each other that we will do the hard work of reconciling, of reconnecting.

One of the ways pornography can damage us is by teaching us that relationships and people are disposable. If you don't like someone, just close the screen and move on to the next.

We carry this toxic form of relating into our real-life relationships. That friend didn't respond the way you felt she should? You stop talking to her. Your accountability partner didn't call when you wanted her to? She's fired. Your pastor says something that rubs you the wrong way, so you leave that church. Your spouse doesn't seem emotionally available, so you give him the cold shoulder.

Every relationship is going to have moments of offense. Sometimes when that happens it is tempting to just burn the bridge and walk away. We all know people who do this. Let me encourage you to pursue healthy conflict resolution and not hold grudges.

When a break in relationship happens, we always have a choice. We need to ask ourselves, *Is this relationship worth fighting for? Is it worth pursuing?* If the answer is yes, then we pursue reconciliation. We try to "make up." If my husband and I disagree, I am going to put in substantial effort to reconcile that relationship because I value it and believe it is absolutely worth fighting for. I have vowed to fight for it.

We, as a human race, offended a holy God—a God we used to have a relationship with. Adam and Eve started it, and thousands of years and billions of beating hearts later, we're continuing it. We continue to offend a holy God with our choices to sin, to define our own truth, to seek our own pleasure, to wound and exploit people who, like us, are created in his image.

In our case, the one who did nothing wrong (God) is pursuing reconciliation with the ones who wronged him (us). God wants that relationship back. We offended him, and yet he doesn't play the part of the offended one. He is the one *pursuing*. The gospel is about that pursuit.

The point of the gospel is not guilt. Jesus didn't suffer so centuries later we would be racked with remorse about his suffering. He suffered for one purpose: reconciliation.

This is the heart of grace and the gospel. God is not fed up with us and wanting us to knock it off. He knows we can't close the gap between us. He bridges it for us and restores us to divine favor. We, as fallen humanity, are in the wrong. He reconciles us to him, even though the most righteous thing any of us could ever do is filthy in his eyes (Isa. 64:6).

That should bring hope to all of us who struggle with sexual sin. God is not pushing us away, disgusted with us. He is not writing us off as lost causes nor standing in heaven screaming at us to stop nailing his son to the cross. His is a message of reconciliation and grace, and it brings satisfaction to his heart. God's desire is not that we get our lives right; it's that we come to him.

The enemy of our souls will do absolutely anything and everything he can to keep us from that relationship. Shame will tell us we are unworthy. Society will tell us it's a relationship we do not need. We will be handed countless ways to avoid, discredit, and discard a relationship with God and blame it on him. *If he weren't so judgmental. If he didn't make me this way. If he hadn't let x, y, z happen. If he would just do something differently. If he would just give me what I want.* But he doesn't, and so we accuse him of breaking the relationship, forgetting that he gave all to be with us.

God's Desire for You

While Jesus is having this conversation with the disciples, the woman is back in her town telling all the people about Messiah. While the disciples are wondering where Jesus picked up takeout, the woman is sharing about her encounter with the Anointed One. She has stood face-to-face with Immanuel—God with us. She has experienced, firsthand, restoration of relationship with the Creator.

And then she leads her town back to Jesus. I picture her leading the townspeople to the well. I doubt they filed neatly down the path. It was probably more like the crowds waiting for the morning train in DC, with people pushing to get ahead of each other, each wanting to be first. I imagine they poured out of the town and across the fields—a literal field of souls ready for reconciliation.

This story takes place near Shechem, a valley in modern Palestine. The valley is filled with springs of water, leading to fertile land rich in agriculture. Even to this day, it boasts a beautiful landscape of fields and vineyards.[2] Jesus's use of a harvest metaphor is a fitting one. Here is a field of humanity coming across the fields, and this is the moment when he tells his disciples the fields are ripe for the harvest.

He says, "Don't you see all of these people ready for me?" It's not a message of condemnation from a frustrated God;

it's a message of hope from a gentle Savior. Jesus talks about rejoicing: "Already the one who reaps is receiving wages and gathering fruit for eternal life, so that sower and reaper may rejoice together" (v. 36 ESV).

I don't often get loud and excited, but if you and I were sitting across from each other in a coffee shop, this is when I might start showing my Baptist roots. This is a truth I just want to shout at the top of my lungs.

God. Wants. A. Relationship. With. You.

God. Desires. You.

We get so stuck in a guilt cycle we even feel bad that God came to save us. Like we could somehow *not* need saving. He knows we need grace, and that's why he gives it.

When it comes to reconciliation, there's no way for you to close the gap. That's not just because you struggle with porn. There's no way for any of us to close the gap. We have all offended God. All of us. You have not unlocked some secret level of offense because you watch pornography.

Porn and Purity Culture

Perhaps we can blame a bit of this confusion of how grace intersects with sexual sin on so-called purity culture. I hit puberty during what I call the "True Love Waits" movement. Purity rings and pledges were a thing. In youth group, girls who lost their virginity were compared to greasy cheeseburgers or chewed-up bubble gum. *Who wants chewed-up bubble gum?*

The message was in order to be desirable to a good, godly person, you needed to be a virgin. If you did not keep your virginity, then you were like chipped china or a flower that had lost all of its petals.

They tried to soften the blow a bit by talking about "secondary virginity." Still, the message was, "If you do this, you are permanently devalued." If this is the message we've heard in the church, is it any wonder that we struggle to believe God would desire us? Why would he when no man ever would?

Or perhaps you've heard the arguments against pornography that center on human exploitation. Maybe you've sat silent while someone screams at the men in the room to get their acts together and stop taking advantage of the women on the screen. After all, that's someone's daughter, for goodness' sake. Maybe you've heard the interviews with serial killers that all seem to tie back to pornography.

Suddenly it's not "just" pornography. Now you're carrying the weight of being a greasy cheeseburger, a human trafficker, and a potential serial killer. No wonder you feel God couldn't possibly desire you. No one would want a relationship with you.

Let me just put a disclaimer here: I disagree with the aggressive tactics adopted in many "break free from porn" programs. Telling me that I'm contributing to human trafficking or am on a glide path toward becoming a sociopath is not going to motivate me toward healing and relationship with God. It might scare me out of doing something or it might light a fire under me and inspire some surge of my will, but it does not deal with any of my underlying issues.

Nor does it draw my heart toward God. It doesn't assure me of his love. If anything, it saddles me with even more guilt, and guilt that never encounters grace is crushing.

God's Desire to Reconcile

God's heart is reconciliation, and we have to trust that. We have to set aside what others have told us about God, or maybe even what we've told ourselves about God, and ask him to reveal his heart for us to us. God doesn't call us greasy cheeseburgers, busted china, or flowers with no petals.

He calls us enemies (Col. 1:21).

Jessica, you're not helping.

Enemies he came not to destroy but to win back. Enemies he had compassion on.

We are led to repentance by his *kindness* (Rom. 2:4).

Enemies he now calls friends, sons, and daughters.

We don't get the grasp of grace until we understand we were enemies of God first. We weren't "frenemies." We weren't distant relatives. We weren't the loners in the back of the class. No, we were enemies. We stood in direct opposition to him. We sided against him. You can't get any more distant and unreconciled than "enemy."

And still Jesus came for us.

He came for *you.*

Even though your choices fly in the face of his design for you. Even though you exploit other people he loves. Even though you are, as Paul says in 1 Corinthians 6:18, sinning against your own body. He came for you.

Forget about heaven and hell, fire and brimstone, for a moment. The gospel is not about "fire insurance." Jesus didn't look out over the field of Samaritans coming to meet him and threaten them. He went back to town and stayed with them for two days.

It's about relationship.

It's about reconciliation.

This truth has to sink into your heart. It forms your new identity. It hands you the keys to your freedom. Any step toward freedom or healing you take is rooted in this reality.

As my old mentor, Sarah, once told me, "You have to love God more than you hate the sin."

We can become obsessed with hating sin, and we give ourselves a list of reasons why what we are doing is bad. We try to use shame and guilt to motivate ourselves to stop. But freedom cannot be motivated by the 101 things that are wrong with pornography. If you're reading this book, you likely don't need anyone to tell you how dark it is. Making the darkness darker doesn't lead us toward the light. It doesn't set us free. It doesn't show us which way to go. It just compounds our feelings of loss and helplessness.

If we want a way out, we need light. The light isn't an accountability partner. It isn't a password protector on the computer. It isn't thirty days without pornography or a twelve-week program. The light is a relationship with Messiah, and he offers this to us freely. He desires us. He desires a relationship with us. Our freedom and continued fight must be rooted in this truth.

His heart is for our reconciliation. His heart is for our freedom. His heart is for us. This is why he came.

I wish I could just pop your heart open and pour this knowledge straight in there. Past all of the mental mazes you're going to try to run it through. You might be thinking of a list of reasons why Jesus couldn't possibly want a relationship with you. Maybe you feel like a fraud. Maybe the type of pornography you watch seems so much worse. Maybe what you do along with pornography makes you feel like a lost cause. Shame is making you question, "But what about [insert obstacle here]?"

Stop trying to talk him out of loving you.

Stop *trying* to talk him out of loving you.

Stop trying to talk *him* out of loving you.

Stop trying to talk him out of *loving* you.

Stop trying to talk him out of loving *you*.

The message of the cross isn't "Look at what you have done to me." It is "Look at what I have done for you." Any freedom worth experiencing starts there. God desires a relationship with each of us. He didn't roll his eyes and begrudgingly save us from our sorry selves. He came to be with us. To be with *you*.

In his encounter with the woman at the well, Jesus walked away satisfied because this was the work he came to do. He came to reconcile a lost and broken world to himself because he loves us. His desire is for us and for a relationship with us.

CHAPTER 10

Living Life Quenched

In November 2016, a small cloud of black smoke billowed over Chimney Tops Mountain in Gatlinburg, Tennessee. Firefighters assessed the threat and believed that the fire had little risk of spreading before incoming rain would put it out. Without intervention, the flames grew slowly but steadily. The rain did not come. A couple of days later, the amount of wind in the forecast increased, so authorities decided to call in three helicopters for a water drop. Things changed dramatically overnight.

That area of Tennessee had experienced a significant drought and, by a geologist's estimation, nearly eighty years of no fires. That meant eighty years' worth of sticks, needles, fallen trees, and leaves waited, now dried, on the forest floor. If you've ever started a fire in a fireplace or while out camping, you may know that these dry materials make great fire starters. Coupled with the high winds, this fire began growing by an estimated half mile per hour.[1] It grew to a fire spreading over seventeen thousand acres, doing millions of dollars' worth of damage, and claiming fourteen lives.[2]

For many of us, pornography and lust feel like wildfire. Maybe your journey started as something small. You downloaded a romance novel. You ventured into a fanfic forum. A friend showed you a video. You just clicked on whatever was trending. It seemed insignificant and unassuming. You felt like you had everything under control. This was nothing more than a phase, just some curiosity, a free-time leisure activity.

Over time, it grew. It might have grown slowly. It might have grown by leaps and bounds. Eventually, you found yourself drawn to new things, more "exciting" things. Your search for new, exciting, and interesting may have become an all-consuming fire, engulfing other areas of your life that have nothing to do with sex. Now you're struggling with anger, trust, concentration, and lack of sleep. Things that seem to have nothing to do with pornography have been set ablaze by it.

What started as a glance at a romance book has morphed into an addiction to hardcore pornography that consumes hours of your time. Years into your journey, you're watching videos that turn your stomach. Recent stats show that categories of pornography that involve bondage, torture, pain, and violence are more popular among women than men.[3] We cannot expect to watch these types of things and remain unscathed.

Your journey may have started with "vanilla" content and now, here you are, watching content that promotes violence toward yourself. What was just something done for entertainment is now a compulsion, something you believe you cannot live without. It can feel like your life is burning out of control.

Or maybe you aren't there yet. Maybe your fire has just started. There's a smoldering on a hill in some distant and disconnected area of your life, and you're trying to convince yourself it's no big deal. It seems easy to contain, and you're pretty sure you could stop if you wanted to—but if you're honest with yourself, you're not sure you want to stop. This tiny little fire doesn't seem like that big of a deal. Until it spreads.

Putting Out Fires

Fires need certain things to grow and spread. In the case of the Gatlinburg fire, plenty of fuel and high winds caused it to become one of the most devastating wildfires in Tennessee's history. But some resources can help us fight and put out fires. One of those things is water.

When Jesus makes the offer of living water in John 4, he tells the woman that the water he offers will "become in them a spring of water welling up to eternal life" (v. 14). I think when some of us picture this idea of Jesus as the living water, it looks less like a spring welling up and more like a water drop from a helicopter. Instead of living life quenched, we live life in constant fire-fighting mode.

Living water becomes the fire hose behind the glass that you break in case of an emergency. You're setting yourself up for an existence riddled with fear and anxiety as you try to stay on guard for the fires. It seems no matter how hard you try, you can never gain the upper hand. The fight never stops.

Put out the fire of pornography. The fire of sex. The fire of lust. The fire of masturbation.

Can water be used to put out fires? Yes. And God is ok with us asking for his help in a time of need (Ps. 46:1), for a way to escape temptation (1 Cor. 10:13), or for wisdom when we're feeling stuck (James 1:5). But if that's the only time we're coming to him, we're missing the point. Putting out fires isn't what it means to live life quenched.

But we tend to live this way. Our first and foremost concern is whether or not our lives are burning to the ground. Talk to certain Christians, and you might get the impression that all God cares about is "behavior modification." They would lead you to believe the main point of the Christian life is to stop doing what you're not supposed to be doing.

If you're stuck in fire-fighting mode, your life will have a familiar pattern. You may walk in perceived freedom for a few days. You're feeling great! You've cleared your history, blocked the sites, unfollowed the accounts, started every day with Bible reading and prayer. Life is good. You stick with your program for a day or two. Maybe even a week, or a month. But slowly, or even suddenly, you get hit with temptation. An errant TikTok video, a fleeting thought, a sexual dream. Next thing you know, you're desperately praying, reciting Bible verses, reaching for anything to stop you as you feel yourself slipping. You shoot a frantic text to your accountability partner, but they don't answer.

Then you fall.

It may be for only a minute, it may be for a couple of hours, but it has happened. You're frustrated, berating yourself. *Nothing works!* You're disgusted with yourself and start beating yourself up. You put the Bible back on the shelf, uninstall the accountability software, and spend a couple of hours, days, or even weeks feeling very stuck and perhaps bingeing on lust.

Then you have a "come to Jesus" moment and pull yourself back together. You reinstall everything, make amends with your accountability partner, and start right back with the same strategy. This time, you're going to try harder. You sign up to be a Bible study leader because you figure that will be good motivation to stay free.

Using God—his grace, love, and goodness—only as a means of quenching fires leaves us with a bunch of dead, burned things. We might not have any fires, but we don't have much of anything else either. We're left with ashes. Some of us believe this is what we have to settle for.

Dry sticks, leaves, and needles are great for starting fires. We call these things kindling. But do you know what makes a lousy fire starter? Anything wet. Wet leaves. Wet wood. Wet paper. If it's wet, it chokes out the fire.

If those mountains in Tennessee had seen their usual rain, the fire would have been less likely to spread as quickly. Water dropped from helicopters may have helped fight the fire, but rain in the months before would have helped *prevent* it.[4]

When we think of breaking free from pornography, almost every step we consider is a form of fire fighting. Password protection, filtering software, accountability apps, and getting rid of our smartphone are all ways to try to douse a fire that is already raging.

What if we could learn to prevent the fire to begin with? What if we could take dry, barren land and have it burst forth with life, new growth, and fruit?

Jesus isn't offering a water drop for us to strategically call in at just the right time. He is offering us a spring. A spring is pure, flowing water that nourishes the land it touches. It penetrates hardened soil, enabling it to bring forth life. It becomes part of the landscape and fundamentally changes it. The closer you are to the spring, the more you experience its benefits. So the greatest work of shame is to cut us off from that spring.

Our Struggle to Rest

In John 15, Jesus compares himself to a vine and us to branches. In verse 4, he says, "Abide in me, and I in you. As the branch cannot bear fruit by itself, unless it abides in the vine, neither can you, unless you abide in me" (ESV). Other Scripture translations read, "Remain in me."

Jesus calls us not to bust our tails trying harder but to remain, to abide, to rest in him. That is where we will find growth and bear fruit. In Galatians 5:16 we are told to "walk by the Spirit," and in doing so we will not gratify our own desires. It's not about putting out fires but about quenching our thirst. We will not find growth or experience new life if all we're doing is using God as a fire extinguisher.

Some of us struggle to rest because all we've known is restlessness. We struggle to feel like we belong because all we've known is the feeling of never being good enough. We can't wrap our minds around this idea of abiding in and remaining in Christ because we find the ideas of safety and community foreign.

The other day, I discovered a note, likely from an old sermon, on my phone. It simply says, "Until we realize our status as part of God's family, we'll live as though we're part of no family at all."

It is so easy for us to live like we're orphans, abandoned and left to our own devices. We flounder around, searching either for something to help us feel whole or something to help us numb our brokenness. When it comes to the heart, we live on the streets, with no place for our hearts and souls to rest. Pornography is a brothel, and we knock on the door in search of warmth, connection, and pleasure, if only for a moment. We believe we belong to ourselves, and so we wander without a sense of belonging, just overwhelming longing.

A Look at Attachment

I've shared before that I grew up in a culture that wasn't a fan of counselors or anything remotely related to the field of mental health. All you needed was Jesus. But in my own journey, I have found great wisdom in understanding what counselors call attachment styles.

Perhaps you've heard of attachment parenting as a way to characterize how some parents choose to nurture their infants. Though initial experiments on attachment theory involved infants and their caregivers, the pioneer of the theory, John Bowlby, always believed adults had the same need for attachment and exhibited the same styles.[5] The idea behind attachment theory is that our attachment to our caregivers as children impacts how we relate to others as adults.

There are four attachment styles; three are considered less than ideal. These unhealthy attachment styles are sometimes given slightly different titles but fall into three classifications based on behaviors: anxious-preoccupied, dismissive-avoidant, and fearful-avoidant.[6]

Those with an anxious attachment style bring a heightened level of anxiety into their relationships. They are very critical of themselves and may need to be constantly reassured and affirmed. They fear abandonment.[7] Instead of security and safety, there is worry and doubt. They feel a desperate need for relationships and yet struggle to truly rest and feel secure in those relationships.

By contrast, those who have developed a dismissive or avoidant attachment style tend to keep their distance. They can be seen as cold or disconnected, even narcissistic, because they prefer to avoid relationships.[8] They are critical of others and are triggered by conflict.[9] Relationships aren't necessarily worth the work for them. They do not have as much anxiety, but the trade-off is fewer relationships overall.

The last of these three styles is disorganized or fearful-avoidant. These are people who want close relationships but are scared of them at the same time.[10] Their relationships can be scenes of emotional chaos. Even as they try to welcome close relationship, the fear of being hurt causes them to push away simultaneously.[11] Nobody is safe, not even themselves.

If you're curious, I fall into this last category. It is a struggle I have known my entire life—wanting so deeply to be known and loved while also fearing the pain such relationships can bring. It often sends me into a tailspin because I want deep relationships but don't want to be hurt by those deep relationships. As a mentor once told me in college, I tend to hold people at arm's length.

Even in my marriage, there are times I have to wrestle with this tendency. While writing this book, I had to sit down with my husband and ask for forgiveness. I realized I had been living these first few years of our marriage in fear. Fear that he would leave. Fear that one day I would finally be too much for him. The fact is, I can't say I trust him while I am secretly afraid he's going to leave. That fear can't coexist with trust.

Attachment and God

Why bring this up? What does any of this have to do with living water, pornography, or living life quenched? Because I believe that how each of us relates to other people can give insight into how we relate to God. Our attachment style can give a glimpse into how shame plays out in our lives.

This isn't meant to provide you with some excuse. Don't walk around now saying, "I have an anxious attachment style, so the world just needs to deal." Instead, see this as a way to identify where healing and growth still need to take place. We cannot abide in the Lord if we aren't secure in our relationship with him. Unhealthy attachment patterns make it difficult to live from a place of security, satisfaction, and rest.

The fourth style of attachment is known as secure attachment. It is marked by a stable and trust-filled view of relationships. In secure attachment, there is a sense of confidence that the relationship will last and has value.[12] People with secure attachment view themselves and others in a positive light.[13]

In *Created for Connection*, Dr. Sue Johnson and Kenneth Sanderfer discuss the need adults have for attachment with others and how this correlates with our attachment with God. Secure attachments are built through responsiveness. Emotional responsiveness is gauged by how we answer three questions: Can I reach you? Can I rely on you to respond to me emotionally? Do I know you will value me and stay close?[14] In secure attachment, the answers are yes, yes, and yes!

How do you answer these three questions in your view of God?

Maybe all of this talk of attachment makes you bristle. It sounds "New Age" to you. You are convinced you must do more. You must try harder. You think God is expecting you to figure this out.

Let me ask you something. Where has that gotten you?

If you're like so many women who struggle, you've been trying to fight this alone—without friends, without family—convinced God wants nothing to do with you. What progress have you made?

We may not have the best role models here on earth. Our parents, lovers, and others who were supposed to care for us may have wounded us in unimaginable ways, creating depths of pain beyond words. But they are not God. They are, at best, a reflection in a dusty, old, broken mirror. Shards of glass that distort the real image while cutting and wounding.

Brokenness has made us feel like we have to do life on our own. We have to figure it out for ourselves. We believe freedom equates to independence, but God's freedom is sourced in dependence. The more dependent we are on him, the freer we become.

Knowing Our Place

Loving Jesus and realizing you are loved by him is perhaps the most important part of your journey. It starts there. Beginning with any other step results in legalism and self-reliance.

This is not about you sprinting across a barren wasteland alone, desperate to get inside the castle walls, with a predator hot on your heels. You are already in the castle, my friend. The life you live now is about keeping the enemy out. It is not about gaining access to living water but rather choosing to drink it and not drink from other cisterns.

When we're living with shame and buying the lies it sells us, we feel like we can never rest. We're never enough. Even in Christian circles, we may hear the message that we have to keep trying. You may believe that. Right now, you may have yourself convinced that a place at this table—a position in God's family—is something you have to fight for. Every morning you wake up, put on your boxing gloves, and get ready for fisticuffs with your struggles. That's not what it means to live life quenched.

Yes, the Bible is full of analogies of war when it comes to sin, but we have to realize where we are fighting from. We don't have to fight to gain our place in the family of God. We fight *from* that place. We fight *from* a place of victory, not defeat. Living life quenched means fighting from a place of belonging, not longing. We don't fight to get *to* a secure place. God has placed us there, and our goal is to remain in it.

As we stay connected to God, he renews our minds. As we abide in him, we grow fruit. He is not the shot of caffeine we need to "make it through" our day. He is the water we need for our very survival, and we have to stay connected to him. Drinking a glass of water now will not quench our thirst forever. We will need more.

We don't just add living water to our lives then walk away completely free and unaffected by pornography and sin. The process takes time. Imagine planting a seed in a parched garden. We plant the seed and then pour water over the soil. That one splash of water is not going to be enough to make that seed sprout, grow, and bring forth fruit. The entire process requires a regular supply of water. I've killed enough houseplants and garden vegetables to confirm this is true. We have to keep watering.

The only way we can prevent the fires of pornography and shame from reducing our hearts to ashes is to stay connected to God.

In an email to her subscribers, author Phylicia Masonheimer lays out four steps for overcoming sexual shame. For her third step, she encourages her readers to "set boundaries out of love, not fear." Why?

> Fear of failure and fear of man . . . lead to legalism or rebellion, and sometimes both. Instead, set boundaries out of love for God and a desire to stay in relationship with Him. This will begin to happen naturally as you ask God to change your heart. Don't just set boundaries without asking "why."[15]

How would your journey change if you started setting up boundaries with the intent of remaining connected to God? So often, our focus on boundaries is about putting out the fires. We're focused on keeping pornography out, but what if we focused on what we are keeping in? What steps can you take to stay connected to, abide in, and rest in Christ? That's where the change will happen.

Our journeys change dramatically when we reframe them through this lens. When I set up boundaries out of love for God, they look different from those I set out of fear he won't love me. I have to believe that I am secure in the love of

God, regardless of what I have done, regardless of the sins I still struggle with, regardless of the lies shame might try to send my way.

Living life quenched means living life secure in the grace and love of God.

Conclusion

Now What?

Do you know something that annoys me? Recipe blogs. They always need to explain the recipe—where it came from, why they decided to make it, what it makes them think of. All I want is the ingredient list and the instructions. My favorite part is the "skip to recipe" button. I overuse it.

When I asked my readers on Instagram what they were looking for in this book, the answer I most frequently received ran along the lines of "Tell me the practical steps for finding freedom." I also talked with my husband about what he felt people were looking for, and his answer was similar: "What are the practical steps for getting free from pornography?"

It's the same sentiment that fills my inbox: "Tell me what I do next."

How do I connect to community when I am so afraid they'll abandon me?

How do I get these images out of my head?

Why do I feel like I can't stop?

What am I supposed to do with my sexual desires?

We want the formulas. We want the steps to follow. We want tangible goals.

Skip to the recipe.

I think, in part, that this desire stems from the feelings of powerlessness and hopelessness we have in our struggles. We've tried. We've tried everything, and so we are on the hunt for the one key ingredient we might be missing. We search for the step-by-step tutorial so we can see where we went wrong.

The Bible is filled with stories of God's grace and how he sets us free, but there are far fewer practical steps for how this works. There is no book in the Bible that details, step-by-step, how to break free from pornography. Quite a few of Jesus's interactions with "sinners" have cliff-hanger endings. In the story of Jesus and the woman at the well, we don't know what happened next in her life. We have no idea what personal steps she put in place.

In John 8, a woman is brought before Jesus after being caught in adultery. Her accusers stand ready to stone her according to the law. Jesus famously says that whoever is without sin should cast the first stone. After all the stones are set down and Jesus and the woman are left alone, he tells her, "Neither do I condemn you; go, and from now on sin no more" (v. 11 ESV).

That story has always left me asking, "How?!"

If I could guarantee that installing a filter on your phone and praying for thirty minutes straight every day would break you free from pornography, your response would likely be a hope-filled, "I can do that!" Steps make us feel strong. Achievable goals generate hope.

But I can't tell you that. No one can. This leaves many women asking an even more important question: "Is freedom even possible?" And, if so, "What does it look like?" and "How do I get there?" You may have even tried the three steps, twelve steps, or forty days someone else promised would work and feel defeated because they didn't.

You're tired of the platitudes. You're weary of people telling you Jesus is enough. He sure doesn't feel like enough. You need answers, and you're here to find them.

You're reading your Bible. You're praying. You've installed the filters. You have the desire to be free. You want freedom more than anything, and you feel desperate, like you're drowning in that desire, unable to get your feet under you and unable to find air.

People think you just aren't trying hard enough, that you truly don't love God enough, that you really don't want freedom. They don't get it. They don't feel the intensity of it all. They don't realize you're likely scared of where this struggle could take you. They don't realize you feel like you're drowning. Wave after wave is pummeling you. You get on top of your struggle only to get sucked under by shame again, and round and round you go.

My primary goal in writing this book was to help pave the way for you to get what you need the most. It might feel like your most pressing need is to get rid of pornography. You tell yourself that if you could only quit, everything else would sort itself out. You want to know how to just stop.

But your most pressing need isn't to get rid of pornography. Your most pressing need is to understand where you stand with Jesus, to realize God's abundant grace for you.

So many messages about breaking free from pornography try to shame you out of your struggle. *Don't you realize you're contributing to human trafficking? Don't you realize that's someone's daughter? Don't you realize pornography is racist, violent, misogynistic, and unhealthy?* And while all of those things can be true, knowing them doesn't bring you any closer to getting out. Freedom isn't found by knowing how ugly and dark pornography is but instead by knowing the grace and beauty found in Jesus.

Our Captive Desires

Once you realize your place in the family of God as his beloved and redeemed daughter, you can begin to wage war against shame. Shame is a thief and a liar, and it is time to take back the ground that shame has tried to steal and tear down the idols it has revealed.

James 1:14–15 lays out the pattern of our struggles:

> Each person is tempted when they are dragged away by their own evil desire and enticed. Then, after desire has conceived, it gives birth to sin; and sin, when it is full-grown, gives birth to death.

It's quite the mental picture here, and one you may feel in the depths of your soul. We are tempted when our own evil desires drag us away. We are lured in and enticed, and then our desires attempt to capture us. This is why, so often, all of our efforts of freedom seem to focus on fighting desire.

But in Proverbs 13:12 "a desire fulfilled is a tree of life" (ESV), and in Psalm 37:4 we read that God will give us the desires of our heart. So, which is it? Is desire going to drown us, or is it going to lead to God-given life?

Dan Allender says,

> Desire lies at the heart of who God made us to be, who we are at our core. Desire is both our greatest frailty and the mark of our highest beauty. Our desire completes us as we become One with our Love, and it separates us from him and brings death as it wars against his will.[1]

Like water, desire can be life-giving or deadly. Like ocean waves, it can be a source of great delight or pull us under. Like a spring of rushing water, it can nourish the land or flood it. Sometimes we may feel powerless to our desires, but the Bible calls us to action.

In 2 Corinthians, Paul reminds us that we have mighty weapons that tear down strongholds. He continues, "We demolish arguments and every pretension that sets itself up against the knowledge of God, and we take captive every thought to make it obedient to Christ" (10:5).

There is a lot of action in this verse. We are demolishing, taking thoughts captive, and making them obedient. This doesn't imply ignorance but intention. We aren't turning a blind eye or just muscling through. We are dealing with these things. Instead of being imprisoned by our errant desires, we are taking them prisoner, and in some cases we are setting them free.

When I read this verse in 2 Corinthians, I imagined putting my errant thoughts in a chokehold and dragging them to Jesus. My prayer life changed drastically when I stopped trying to ignore the pornographic memories popping up in my head and started calling them out. My marriage changed for the better when I shared moments of temptation with my husband so we could pray over them together.

When it comes to your desires, my challenge to you is to take them captive and bring them to Jesus. This may feel backward, because our impulse is to run from our temptations, not sit down and conduct an interview with them. In his book *Unwanted*, Jay Stringer says, "Your sexual struggles reveal your wounds, but they also reveal the trafficked longings of your heart."[2]

Sometimes those desires need to be renewed to their original intent, like the renewing of our minds Paul mentions in Romans 12:2. Sometimes our desires point to places where we need healing. Sometimes they point to gods that need to be uprooted. Sometimes they expose areas where shame is still haunting our hearts.

Throughout these pages, we've talked about different desires we have and how shame can thwart them. If we are able to fight to bring those desires back to where God wants them, we will effectively undo the damage of shame and rob it of its power. We can set our captive desires free by acting on the truth of God's Word. As we do that, I believe we set ourselves up to be able to walk in freedom from pornography and live a life quenched.

The Desire to Be Known

One part of the John 4 story I find so telling is that the woman, once she met Jesus, went *back to her town*. She went back to her community. Her testimony to that community was that Jesus knew everything about her.

When Jesus first encountered the woman at the well, she was quick to remind him of the cultural expectations of the day. She knew who she was, but he had apparently forgotten the rules. If he knew who he was talking to, well, he wouldn't be talking to her.

Shame takes our desire to be known and causes us to fear it, driving us into isolation and hiding. Grace redeems that desire and welcomes us into open, authentic community with God *and* with others.

For years now, when a woman has asked me for the first step she should take when she's trying to break free, my answer has been, "You need to tell someone." Not so they can shame you but rather help prove shame wrong.

This is an unpopular opinion in some circles, but I don't like the word *accountability*. I don't like the idea of having a relationship with someone that centers completely on whether or not I am committing a certain behavior. There is no model of "accountability partners" in the Bible, at least not in the way we practice it. I believe some of our accountability models can perpetuate shame instead of eradicating it. That's why I don't encourage accountability but instead *community*.

As I mentioned earlier, I had a team of women around me when I was breaking free from pornography. Of that team, *only one* would ask me questions about my struggle with pornography. The rest of the women focused on all of the areas of my life where I needed growth and healing. And while that team is no longer in place, through the years I have continued to find growth and healing in various areas of my life through Christian community.

These communities have never focused on my struggle with pornography. In fact, in recent years there are only two people who I would say are my "accountability partners," and they also happen to be two of my best friends, one being my husband.

I would argue that no relationship in your life, even a counseling one, should be solely focused on pornography, because there is more to you than the videos you watch online.

Oftentimes when women tell me, "There's no one I can tell," they are either saying they don't have a community or they don't trust their community. Don't fool yourself. Community you don't trust isn't community. If you would say, "There's no one I can tell," then my answer to you is to pray for God to help you build a community or to tear down your idol of self-image, whichever it might be.

The Desire to Be Loved

Healthy community also helps speak to another desire—the desire to be loved. When shame intersects with this desire, it tells us we are unable to be loved. That, in turn, shakes our identity and our security in our relationships. Remember that part of living life quenched is living life resting, secure, and abiding in the love of God. We can't do that if we think we're unlovable.

This is why I feel it's important to share your story with people who know you. If you only involve strangers or manage to break free on your own, then you will continue to wonder if people in your life could really love you. *Would they still love me if they knew?* That's the question shame wants to plant deep in your heart.

Do you feel it?

I could never tell my parents. They would be so ashamed.

I am never going to be able to be married because of this.

If I tell my husband, I just know he'll leave.

No one could ever really want me.

Pornography couples with shame to take captive and even attempt to kill your desire to be loved. Pornography will try to tell you how to be loved. It will change what love looks like. It sexualizes love and then introduces violence. The tenderness and sweetness of love are replaced by a self-serving, bitter sexuality that is never satisfied. Love and sex become so entwined and twisted that we simply can't separate the two or understand a love that doesn't demand sexually. In turn, we have a hard time loving others well and accepting others' love well.

We have to remember that love is not what happens in the bedroom. *Even in marriage.* Love transcends all of this. Perhaps it's cliché, but spend some time reflecting on 1 Corinthians 13, affectionately known as "the love chapter." It's popular at weddings and probably in some February sermon series, but there is some conviction in there. Love is not proud. *Ouch.* Love does not keep a record of wrongs. *Strike two.*

This is, again, where healthy community is so important. In a healthy community, we can learn to love and be loved in a way that has nothing to do with sex.

About That Sexual Desire

Well, then, you might be asking, *what am I supposed to do about sex?*

I get it. I got married when I was thirty-two, and I was a virgin. For nearly two decades I asked God what exactly I was supposed to do with my sex drive. It felt like I'd been handed the keys to a shiny new car and then told I wasn't allowed to drive it. *Then why give me the keys?!*

In our frustration and struggle with pornography, it can be easy for us to view our sex drive as the problem. If we didn't have one, then this wouldn't be an issue, right? Therefore we decide the real enemy here is our sexual desires.

We try to ignore them. We don't talk about them. We smother them in shame in hopes they'll be extinguished. Unfortunately, the purity culture has been party to this as well. But all of these tactics ignore what is really going on when we're watching pornography.

Some classify pornography as a supernormal stimulus. This means that all of the feel-good feelings we get from pornography are far more than what we get from sex. Because of this, over time our bodies begin to crave pornography, not just sex. In essence, pornography can hijack our God-given sex drive and replace it with somewhat of a "pornography drive." That means "killing our sex drive" isn't going to help. It's already dying. We don't want to kill it; we need to *rescue* it.

This is going to sound absurd, but one of the best ways to do this is to start having healthy conversations about sex. You don't fight lies with silence, you silence them with truth.

Let me start by telling you that you are allowed, as a Christian woman, to desire and enjoy sex. Our bodies are designed to enjoy sexual pleasure. There is nothing wrong or sinful about that. Pornography didn't make you that way. The sexual revolution didn't either. God did. You are not "weird" because you want to have sex. The answer to rescuing your sexual desires isn't to ignore them but to recall them for all they are supposed to be.

This is, by far, one of the trickiest desires to get back from shame. I would encourage you to do this with a counselor, because pornography can thwart our views of love, introduce trauma into sex, and just make a big mess of everything. Then, on the other hand, we have Christian communities where sex is never allowed to be discussed. We're left with a tangled knot and it honestly just seems easier to throw it all away.

Here, again, we see the importance and value of a healthy Christian community. In a community of other Christian women, I can have honest conversations about sex. That's not a pie-in-the-sky dream but a reality. I, Jessica, have a community in which I can have open and honest conversations about sex, and that's not just because I write about it. Has it always been this way? No. Do I talk openly about sex in every one of my communities? No. Boundaries and discernment are absolutely important, but if you want to disconnect shame and sex, you can't be ashamed to talk about sex.

The Desire to Worship

When we are able to rightly understand our desire to be loved, this has a profound impact on how we worship. When I introduced the concept of shame in chapter 2, I shared some insights from Dan Allender and Tremper Longman about the way shame reveals our idols. The areas of our lives in which we feel the most shame are likely where our idols are hiding in the shadows.

Just the other day, I sat in a women's Bible study as we discussed the story of the rich young ruler in Luke. Here was a young man who had it all and, by his own recollection, had kept all the rules. He asked what he still needed to inherit eternal life, and Jesus told him he needed to sell everything he had. The ruler went away sad.

This story made me think of what it means for us to follow Jesus. As a Christian in America, I recognize that my faith and practice of it are pretty comfortable. I can meet in a church building knowing that the government protects my right to do so. In other countries, Christians meet in secret locations because the government will punish them for their faith. I can admit that my idea of worship is a rather cheap one at times. It can be a bit of a spectator sport, and it doesn't cost me anything.

As I wrote this book, I asked women to share their stories. One woman who struggled with lust, masturbation, and "mommy porn" shared a turning point for her on her journey of freedom.

> *I also needed to want Jesus more than freedom. I remember telling Him, "Even if I have to battle this the rest of my life, I still want You." After months of that intense battle, including what felt like some of my worst failures and darkest hours, He broke through and set me free. . . . After that happened, the Lord showed me that my biggest hurdle was not sexual sin at all but [rather] turning to other things and people for comfort and to numb pain or emotions that I couldn't process. Out of habit, that would lead to sexual sin. I was willing to give up sexual sin, but deep down was not willing to give up my comforts.*

That opening line of her testimony strikes me as so profound. She needed to want Jesus more than freedom. Do you want Jesus more than freedom? So many of our strategies and tricks and tips for freedom are focused solely on freedom.

We can even approach things like Bible study and prayer as a trick to try to break free. Do you want Jesus more?

Since we've already talked about worship and what it can look like, I want to ask you this: Is there something you are unwilling to give up in your journey for freedom?

My husband often counsels men who struggle with pornography. Occasionally, he will encourage a man to give up his phone or his computer or to just stop watching pornography. The response is often, "No, I can't do that."

I want to encourage you to go through a list of your comforts. Are they keeping you comfortable in your struggle? What if God were to ask you to give up your cell phone or to delete your social media accounts? What if you should get rid of your boyfriend or delay that wedding date? What if you should step down from a ministry position?

If you feel yourself saying, "No, I can't do that," then you may have just exposed an idol.

In Romans 13, Paul says, "Let us walk properly as in the daytime, not in orgies and drunkenness, not in sexual immorality and sensuality, not in quarreling and jealousy. But put on the Lord Jesus Christ, and *make no provision for the flesh*, to gratify its desires" (vv. 13–14 ESV).

The Desire for Healing

Have you ever noticed that shame likes to masquerade as safety and protection? We all have areas of our lives that are wounded and broken. Areas where we need to know the healing power of Jesus. Places of brokenness in desperate need of his grace. Shame calls us not into healing but into hiding.

A couple years ago, my husband injured his back at work. He went to physical therapy to help strengthen it. The doctors told him it would never be 100 percent, but putting in the work would help alleviate the pain, and he'd have an easier time with day-to-day activities. He noticed on days when he had physical therapy or worked out that his back would be sore the next day. When our schedule didn't allow, he would sometimes go for weeks without one of his back strengthening workouts. During those weeks, he wouldn't experience any soreness or discomfort. This led him to wonder if the physical therapy was somehow making it worse.

It wasn't, of course; the soreness he experienced from physical therapy was actually a healthy sign of muscle strengthening. He realized this after several months of workouts when he was able to lift heavier weights and work out longer than he had previously.

Healing is work. It can be uncomfortable work. Nobody likes walking down broken paths. Nobody enjoys rehashing painful memories. It's not necessarily fun.

Shame can tell you it isn't worth it and will reframe your desire for healing as something to be feared or ignored. You might call yourself high maintenance or needy. Shame will try to tell you that it's not worth bringing up, and you're just going to have to deal with it.

As someone who has been there, and in many ways is still there, let me encourage you that healing is worth it—even though it is hard work and it can be painful to open up those places that need to be touched by God's redemptive love and grace.

Please don't believe you have to keep those places closed off. Please don't believe God is not interested in your healing. This goes, again, back to community, but *tell somebody*. And give yourself permission to pursue healing.

Shame likes to pretend it is keeping us safe. Shame tells us that staying in the dark keeps us from getting our hearts broken. It keeps us from being exposed. It keeps us from being embarrassed or hurt. Shame tells us that the safest place for us is to hide. But grace calls us into the light to be known and to showcase God's love.

The Call of Grace

This is what I hope you see as we wrap this all up. I hope you see grace. I hope you see it shining like a light, beckoning you to walk in the light. To walk in freedom.

In chapter 1, I shared the stories of women who were "at the well." These women felt absolutely trapped by their struggle with pornography. Let me share the rest of their stories with you.

Esther began a friendship with some ladies in her online church group. During a church prayer meeting, she asked for prayer for an addiction. One of the women reached out to her privately to see what was going on. Esther took the opportunity to share that she had struggled with pornography for years. The response was not at all what she expected. These women came alongside her and supported her, praying and fasting with her. Esther began to experience freedom and victory.

Jamie's journey to freedom was complicated by the existence of abuse within her close circles and a history of bad relationships and unhealthy boundaries. So she chose to share her story in the safety of a counseling setting. In her words,

I am actually able to say no now. I continue to feel tempted to this day, and there have been times I slipped

up. But I have also been able to approach my husband to confess what I did and process the temptation with him. This is different from before.

I think the thing I always have to remember about my pornography use is that I am never above it. Even when I think I am done struggling with it, I am not. I need to take the precautions to keep me from falling. I am still trying to nail this down. But more than anything, the freedom is found in Christ who has set me free. It is found in his great love for me, that he still loves me even in the midst of my sin.

The most helpful Scripture for me is Hebrews 4:14–16. These verses and the experience of receiving grace from my Christian community when I have shared that I struggle with pornography have challenged my view that God is angry with me, thinks I am dirty, and wants nothing to do with me. This passage challenges me to stop trying to clean myself up but instead, in the midst of my mess, to run to God because he is the only one who can help me and provide me what I need to fight temptation. And he can empathize with me because he lived like we did, yet he did it perfectly.

And finally, Charlotte's story. After her initial email to me, I encouraged her to reach out to a counselor who specialized in sexual trauma. When I asked for permission to share her story, this is the update she gave:

I wonder why I never responded [to you]. It feels like so long ago. I have been going to therapy since then. I even did EMDR therapy. I do not struggle with pornography anymore, and I have a real relationship with God now. There are still things I struggle with pertaining to the abuse, and healing is never easy. [I am] grateful that you emailed me. It was the reminder I needed.

Grace calls us to connection and community; shame tells us to fear them.

Grace calls us to confession; shame tells us we can't.

Grace gives us a new identity; shame continues to call us by our failures.

If grace is calling us into community and connection, and shame is telling us to fear them, then fighting shame looks like pressing even harder into community and connection. If grace is calling us to share our story, then fighting shame means doing just that. When God gives us a new identity, fighting shame looks like choosing to claim it and walk in it. In the words of Jay Stringer, "Shame is certainly a terrifying beast, but each time we choose not to live as its prey, we find it less powerful than we imagined."[3]

When it comes to dealing with our desires, we have to be determined to demolish the wall of shame that is attempting to protect them. We have to clear the way for God to do his work of redemption and restoration. We have to be willing to give up our comforts—both material and emotional.

We do so not out of fear or need to earn our position but because God himself offers the greatest comfort. He offers greater satisfaction and abundant life.

Every action you take—from installing software to burning novels to sharing your story—should be motivated not by shame or guilt but by love . . . and desire. Desire is not the enemy. If anything, shame is the enemy, and always has been. But where shame demands a sweltering walk alone to a well, God offers us a spring of living water and abundant life, a long walk redeemed, and captive desires set free.

Drink in, friend, and let your thirst be quenched.

A Special Letter to Those Who Don't Struggle

If a struggle with pornography or lust isn't part of your story, you may be wondering how you fit into this narrative. Perhaps you picked up this book because you know a woman who is struggling and want to help. Maybe you are just curious and want to learn.

You can choose one of two roles in the life of a woman who needs help. You can offer assistance, clearing the way for God to work in her life, or you can stand back and judge. In my life, I have experienced both.

In college, when I was first caught in pornography, I was told that women couldn't have this problem. There was no grace. No help. No hope. The dean of women reprimanded me for handing out my password to male friends on campus, even though that isn't what happened. I was made to sign a contract saying I would never share my password again, and the conversation ended there.

This experience left me broken and without hope. I gave up and, in one day, traded in my dreams of being a doctor for settling for life as a porn star.

That dean's words opened up a pit of shame and despair in my life.

A year later, at a new college, a different conversation took place. There, the dean of women stood in front of a room full of young Christian women and said, "We know some of you struggle with pornography and masturbation, and we're here to help you."

That conversation was a shining light of hope that cut through the fog in my heart. When I confessed, they met me with grace. They could have told me I was disgusting, disgraceful, and unworthy. Instead, they called my confession *brave*. They spoke the truth, and it was the truth that set me free.

It took nearly two years of counseling and discipleship for me to finally feel like I was free. For a while, every time I went back home on break, I would spend my days entrenched in pornography again. Breaking that cycle took longer than I ever thought it would.

The best thing that happened in my journey of freedom was the team of women who helped me see who I am without pornography. As pornography's hold on my life lessened, I found my footing in my identity in Christ.

When the problem of lust is addressed in Christian circles, it is almost always made a male issue. The pronoun "he" infiltrates the conversation. Parents address pornography and lust with their sons. Men's breakfasts are devoted to the topic of men and pornography. Dress codes are written on the principle that men struggle with lust and women shouldn't cause their brothers to stumble.

But when it comes to the struggle women can face, the halls fall silent. Women's events don't center on pornography and lust; they focus on true beauty and being a good wife. As women struggle alone, in silence, smothered in shame, we hold hope out to them but fail to let them know they can have it.

Even if you don't think you know a woman who struggles with lust, odds are you do. And even if you don't know who she is, you have an opportunity to extend hope to her by changing the conversation. It's relatively simple and only requires the word *and*.

When you talk about pornography, in whatever sphere of influence you have, the new conversation looks like this:

Men and women struggle with pornography, lust, and masturbation.
Men and women struggle with erotica and porn.
Men and women struggle with their heart and their eyes.
Parents should talk to their sons and daughters.

A woman who struggles is waiting. She is listening. She is holding out hope that someone, somewhere, will know she exists and will tell her she is not alone.

Several years back, women from my church began coming to me to share their stories. Women fighting wars against lust and pornography, chained down by guilt, shame, and crushing feelings of isolation. One after another, they reached out and asked to meet with me. One by one, they shared their stories over coffee at a local restaurant or while sitting in my living room. Each woman bared her heart and shared this one theme: "I thought I was alone."

The truly heartbreaking realization came for me when I found out some of these women were in the same small group. They were already in fellowship with one another, sitting in Bible study together but convinced that this problem was too big, too ugly, too weird to share. They were suffering in silence right next to someone else suffering in silence.

More recently, I sat in a small group of eight women all reading a sheet of paper. A woman in the group had written out her story because it was too hard for her to voice. It was a story of addiction to pornography rooted in sexual trauma, and she sat, with face flushing, as we read it. She then tried to rush the conversation along, like someone trying to slam the lid on an overstuffed suitcase. I stopped her.

"I want to tell you that you are brave, and you are not alone."

The redness in her cheeks went away, and she exhaled. What followed was one of the most powerful Bible studies I have ever been privileged to take part in as women around the room shared their stories—stories of sexual abuse, stories of struggles with mental health caused by shame and guilt.

One woman even said, "I don't usually share this with anyone, but it helps to know I am not alone."

The conversation about pornography and lust has to change. Even if you don't personally know a woman who struggles, you can be a part of changing that conversation.

You have the opportunity to change the conversation both in the life of one woman and in the church overall.

You don't have to have the same background as whomever you are trying to help. You don't have to have firsthand experience with what she is experiencing. The only requirement to be able to help a woman who is struggling is to know truth and to speak it.

Speak the truth about the struggle women have. Speak the truth about the grace God has for them. Speak the truth that there is redemption and there is hope and she is never too far gone. Speak the truth that, no matter what her story, she is not alone.

It doesn't matter if pornography is part of your story. You don't need to know the darkness to lead someone to the light.

Too often, we forget God's heart of redemption and reconciliation. You don't have to know where the prodigal has been in order to be able to lead them home.

Setting Up a Recovery Community

People who are looking for help breaking free from pornography already want to stop. That's why they're looking for help. Many are desperately trying to find the solution. They are looking for practical resources, answers, and support to help them take the steps they need to experience freedom. As a church, we have the opportunity to shepherd people along that journey to freedom. An effective way to do this is to set up support or recovery groups. I like to call them community groups, but you can brand them however you would like.

Support and recovery groups are a practical way for us to help encourage women on their walk of freedom. Here are five steps to setting one up.

1. Find a Good Leader

Any group is only as strong and healthy as the person leading it. A women's recovery group should be facilitated by a woman who is passionate about helping women find healing and freedom. She should be trustworthy and discerning. No woman is going to trust and open up to a known gossip or judgmental person. Likewise, no man should facilitate a women-only group. Choose a leader you trust, because you are going to need to trust her.

She does not have to have prior experience with this struggle. So many pastors and leaders fall into the trap of believing that they need to find a woman who used to struggle with porn to lead a group of women who struggle with porn. That is not the case. Why? Because these groups should be more about where you are going and less about where you are or have been.

That being said, once you start opening the discussion about the issue of women struggling with pornography, you may find leaders naturally emerge. You never know until you ask.

Don't simply reach out to some woman in leadership or the wife of someone in leadership because she seems like a great fit. Let God call the leader; not you.

2. Determine the Mission

What is the point of the group? Is it going to be an eight-week study and then the group will dissolve? Is it going to be something more long-term? Is it a program women "graduate" from, or is it a community they can be a part of indefinitely? Is the point intensive recovery, or is it more a form of support?

Those are questions you need to answer based on what resources are available to you and your people. Each has its own benefits, but the important thing is that the group has a defined and clear mission from the start. What is the purpose, and how are you planning to accomplish it? What materials or resources are you going to use?

One of the pitfalls of support groups is that they can become sounding boards instead of places of growth. They are not meant to be a place where members can meet up just to talk about pornography. That becomes a club where everyone is trying to outdo everyone else's story, or people are more interested in "getting things off their chest" than they are in actually healing.

Defining the purpose and mission of the group from the beginning helps keep it on track. Likewise, setting a fixed time (eight weeks, six months, one year) gives clear expectations and builds in an opportunity to reevaluate. If things aren't working after six months, you have an opportunity to pause, reassess, and try a different approach if needed.

3. Be Discreet

Yes, you are being open and honest about the fact that Christian women struggle with porn. However, when you are setting up this group, exercise a bit of discretion. Do not, for instance, put an announcement in your bulletin calling for all women who struggle to come forward to the front after church for a brief meeting. Do not post a sign outside of the classroom door saying, "Support for women who struggle with pornography." Have the group meet in someone's home or off-hours at the church. Do not advertise the meeting place or time. Instead, have women reach out to the leader individually to discuss joining the group and to receive more information. This helps to make women feel more comfortable and also protects them from would-be predators.

4. Establish Confidentiality

Have members of the group commit to confidentiality. They are not to disclose who is in the group or what is talked about in the group. This includes the leader. For this reason, having two women colead may be very beneficial, as they will be able to talk things through with each other.

You may draw up a contract of sorts, a promise of commitment and confidentiality. If it is an eight-week course, for instance, you may have each member commit to attending all eight weeks as a condition of joining the group. Additionally, she agrees not to disclose who is in attendance or what others have shared. She is always welcome to share what she is learning, but should never disclose personally identifying information or stories from other people in the group.

5. Have Backup

Unless you are a certified counselor, you are not a certified counselor. The woman leading your group is likely not a certified counselor (though if you have one who is willing to lead a group like this, jump on that!).

These sorts of groups can uncover lots of brokenness and pain. They can unearth sexual trauma, abandonment issues, suicidal thoughts, body image issues, and so much more. It's not your job or your group facilitator's job to fix any of that. Be willing to admit when you are in over your head and have a backup to whom you can refer people. You may even ask that counselor to show up one week just to introduce herself and to schedule preliminary appointments with any women who would like one.

Additionally, have your group facilitator meet with a counselor as a condition of leading the group. Leading groups like this and hearing other people's stories can wear on someone. She is going to need a healthy place to be able to discuss that with someone who has the same commitment to confidentiality and has no skin in the game.

As you embark on this journey of setting up support groups for women in your church, here are some important points to remember:

Take care of your leaders. This can be emotionally exhausting work. Check in on them and be sure they are not taking on too much.

Not every woman will come forward the first time. Be willing to start small and try this twice.

The purpose of these groups isn't "to get women to stop watching pornography." It's to have women experience freedom, healing, and the abundant life God promises them.

Freedom takes time. Do not expect a 100 percent success rate at the end of a ten-week course. In my journey, it took well over a year before I would say I experienced freedom. Factor that reality into your expectations for this group.

Acknowledgments

Speaking of community.

I almost always read the acknowledgments first. What can I say? I *really* like skipping to the end! As a teenager, when I would get a new CD, I would open the jacket and flip through until I found the part where the artist said thank you to all of the important people in their life who helped make the work happen. Such thank-yous communicate a sense of belonging, of being part of a journey to something bigger.

Writing is certainly a journey, and it is never done alone. The road from thought to written word to published word is long and winding, and I am thankful for those who have walked along the road with me.

Michael, we did it! Years ago when we made our vows, one part spoke to my heart more than all the others: "and will join with you on the mission God has entrusted to us." Your name isn't on the cover, but, my love, your imprint is all over this book. Thank you for championing the dreams

God has placed on my heart. These pages are, in part, the result of your prayers, love, and encouragement. Thank you for corralling our girls so I could write. You are an amazing husband and father, and will always be one of the greatest evidences of grace in my life.

Laney, Frankie, and the Smith family, what unspeakable blessings you are in such a crazy time. Thank you for loving our little girls and making it so I could get these words on paper without losing too much sleep.

My illustrious agent, Mary, from Switzerland until now—what a ride. I can write hard stories because women like you went before. You believed in this message when I felt like letting it fade away. You are more than an agent. You are a prayer warrior, a mentor, and a dear friend.

To the Baker Books team—Patnacia, Rachel, Hannah, Brianna, Jessica, Lindsey, and many others I'm sure I never got to "meet"—thank you for believing in this book and making it what it is. You believed in the vision and brought it to life in ways I never could have.

Amanda from The Victory Collective, thank you for helping me craft this content to reach our mission field. I am so grateful for the work you're doing. Do not grow weary.

To Sam and the team at Covenant Eyes. You all have been there pretty much since day one. Thank you for your support and for giving voices a platform. Let's change the culture together.

To my friends and prayer warriors—Abby, Tabetha, Mary, Loriel, Tammy, Kurt, Jake, Jessie, Grace, Hannah, and so many others—God has used you to show me more of his heart and the power of authenticity in community.

And while it seems cliché to leave this for last, it seems fitting for it to be the final word. Thank you, Jesus. Every story begins and ends with you. Without you, the story would end differently for all of us. Thank you for coming for us. May every word in these pages point hearts to their home in you.

Notes

Chapter 1 Cries from the Well

1. "Pornography Statistics," Covenant Eyes, accessed June 1, 2022, https://www.covenanteyes.com/pornstats.

2. Kimberly Amadeo, "What Are the Odds of Winning the Lottery?," The Balance, October 24, 2021, https://www.thebalance.com/what-are-the-odds-of-winning-the-lottery-3306232.

3. "Preventable Deaths: Odds of Dying," National Safety Council, accessed June 1, 2022, https://injuryfacts.nsc.org/all-injuries/preventable-death-overview/odds-of-dying/.

4. Ingrid Solano, Nicholas R. Eaton, and K. Daniel O'Leary, "Pornography Consumption, Modality and Function in a Large Internet Sample," *Journal of Sex Research* 57, no. 1 (2018): 92–103, https://doi.org/10.1080/00224499.2018.1532488.

5. Josh McDowell Ministry and Barna Group, *The Porn Phenomenon* (Ventura, CA: Barna, 2016), 32–33.

Chapter 2 The Long Walk to the Well

1. Brené Brown, "Shame v. Guilt," Brené Brown, January 15, 2013, https://brenebrown.com/blog/2013/01/14/shame-v-guilt/.

2. James F. McGrath, "Ask a Scholar: Woman at the Well," Bible Odyssey, accessed June 1, 2022, https://www.bibleodyssey.org:443/en/tools/ask-a-scholar/woman-at-the-well.

3. Chandler Vinson, "Five Husbands?!?! (John 4:18)," *A Trivial Devotion* (blog), January 29, 2014, https://trivialdevotion.blogspot.com/2014/01/five-husbands-john-418.html.

4. D. A. Carson, R. T. France, and J. A. Motyer, eds., *New Bible Commentary*, 21st century ed. (Downers Grove, IL: InterVarsity, 1994), 1033.

5. Dan Allender and Tremper Longman III, *The Cry of the Soul: How Our Emotions Reveal Our Deepest Questions about God* (Colorado Springs: NavPress, 2015), 171.

6. Allender and Longman, 172.

7. Allender and Longman, 174.

8. Allender and Longman, 177.

9. Allender and Longman, 195–96.

Chapter 3 The Desire to Be Known

1. R. Alan Culpepper, *The Gospel and Letters of John* (Nashville: Abingdon, 1998), 139.

2. Julye Bidmead, "Places: Women and Wells in the Hebrew Bible," Bible Odyssey, accessed June 1, 2022, https://www.bibleodyssey.org:443/en /places/related-articles/women-and-wells-in-the-hebrew-bible.

3. Leslie Vernick, *The Emotionally Destructive Relationship: Seeing It, Stopping It, Surviving It* (Eugene, OR: Harvest House, 2007), 56.

Chapter 4 The Desire to Be Free

1. Strong's Concordance, s.v. "2198, *zaó*," Biblehub.com, accessed July 1, 2022, https://biblehub.com/greek/2198.htm.

2. J. W. McGarvey and Philip Y. Pendleton, "The Fourfold Gospel: At Jacob's Well, and at Sychar Commentary," Bible Study Tools, accessed June 1, 2022, https://www.biblestudytools.com/commentaries/the-fourfold -gospel/by-sections/at-jacobs-well-and-at-sychar.html.

3. Mo Isom Aiken, *Fully Known: An Invitation to True Intimacy with God* (Grand Rapids: Baker Books, 2021), 59.

Chapter 5 The Desire to Be Loved

1. Fred H. Wight, "Manners & Customs: Water Supply," Ancient Hebrew Research Center, accessed June 1, 2022, https://www.ancient-hebrew.org /manners/water-supply.htm.

2. Josh McDowell and Ben Bennett, *Free to Thrive: How Your Hurt, Struggles, and Deepest Longings Can Lead to a Fulfilling Life* (Nashville: Thomas Nelson, 2021), 18–32.

3. Brent Curtis and John Eldredge, *The Sacred Romance: Drawing Closer to the Heart of God* (Nashville: Thomas Nelson, 1997), 31.

4. Jay Stringer, *Unwanted: How Sexual Brokenness Reveals Our Way to Healing* (Colorado Springs: NavPress, 2018), 41.

5. Juli Slattery, *Rethinking Sexuality: God's Design and Why It Matters* (Portland: Multnomah, 2018), 26.

6. Stringer, *Unwanted*, 6.

7. Aiken, *Fully Known*, 65.

8. Ellen Dykas, ed., *Sexual Sanity for Women: Healing from Sexual and Relational Brokenness* (Greensboro: New Growth Press, 2012), 86.

Chapter 6 The Desire to Worship

1. John Piper, "What Is Worship?," Desiring God, April 29, 2016, https://www.desiringgod.org/interviews/what-is-worship.

2. Mo Isom Aiken, *Sex, Jesus, and the Conversations the Church Forgot* (Grand Rapids: Baker Books, 2018), 43.

3. Phylicia Masonheimer, *Stop Calling Me Beautiful* (Eugene, OR: Harvest House, 2020), 52.

4. Slattery, *Rethinking Sexuality*, 116.

Chapter 7 The Desire for Healing

1. Psalm 77:13; Isaiah 6:3; Revelation 15:4.

2. Job 37:23; Psalm 89:14; Proverbs 24:12.

3. Psalm 103:8–14.

4. James 1:5.

5. Dykas, *Sexual Sanity*, 88.

6. Staci Sprout, "Porn Harms Girls in 12 Ways: Fight Back with 3 Empowering Mindsets," Defend Young Minds, December 7, 2021, https://www.defendyoungminds.com/post/porn-harms-girls-12-ways-fight-back-3-empowering-mindsets.

7. "How Porn Can Change the Brain," Fight the New Drug, accessed June 1, 2022, https://fightthenewdrug.org/how-porn-can-change-the-brain.

Chapter 8 A Long Walk Redeemed

1. Liz Curtis Higgs, "The Woman at the Well: Thirsty for Truth," *Today's Christian Woman*, July 2008, https://www.todayschristianwoman.com/articles/2008/july/woman-at-well.html.

2. McDowell and Bennett, *Free to Thrive*, 126.

Chapter 9 A Desire Satisfied

1. McDowell and Bennett, *Free to Thrive*, 108–9.

2. "Topical Bible: Shechem," Bible Hub, accessed June 1, 2022, https://biblehub.com/topical/s/shechem.htm.

Chapter 10 Living Life Quenched

1. "Mountain Firestorm: The Story of the Gatlinburg Wildfires," YouTube video, 16:19, posted by Knoxville News Sentinel, November 19, 2017, https://youtu.be/sJL_2qfH7BY.

2. "NewsChannel 5 Documentary: Fire On The Mountain," YouTube video, 22:53, posted by NewsChannel 5, February 24, 2017, https://youtu.be/nbW1xbLwaic.

3. "What Kind of Porn Do Women Watch?" Fight the New Drug, July 30, 2021, https://fightthenewdrug.org/how-do-men-and-womens-porn-site-searches-differ/.

4. "NewsChannel 5 Documentary: Fire On The Mountain."

5. Sue Johnson with Kenneth Sanderfer, *Created for Connection: The "Hold Me Tight" Guide for Christian Couples* (New York: Little, Brown Spark, 2016), 27.

6. Jessica Anderson, "What Are the Four Attachment Styles?" Better-Help, April 20, 2022, https://www.betterhelp.com/advice/attachment/what-are-the-four-attachment-styles.

7. Dennis Relojo-Howell, "Types of Attachments, According to Attachment Theory," Psychreg, September 18, 2021, https://www.psychreg.org/types-attachment-attachment-theory/.

8. Anderson, "What Are the Four Attachment Styles?"

9. Aundi Kolber, *Try Softer: A Fresh Approach to Move Us out of Anxiety, Stress, and Survival Mode—and into a Life of Connection and Joy* (Wheaton: Tyndale, 2020), 57.

10. Anderson, "What Are the Four Attachment Styles?"

11. Kolber, *Try Softer*, 57.

12. Anderson, "What Are the Four Attachment Styles?"

13. "Secure Attachment—from Childhood to Adult Relationships," The Attachment Project, July 2, 2020, https://www.attachmentproject.com/blog/secure-attachment/.

14. Johnson and Sanderfer, *Created for Connection*, 60–61.

15. Phylicia Masonheimer, Lust Free Living, "Day Two: Overcoming Sexual Shame," email distribution list, September 18, 2021.

Conclusion Now What?

1. Dan B. Allender, *To Be Told: God Invites You to Coauthor Your Future* (Colorado Springs: Waterbrook, 2006), 47–48.

2. Stringer, *Unwanted*, 35.

3. Stringer, 145.

About the Author

If you've read this book, then you already know more about me than I ever wanted people to know. It's always strange for me to think that I can walk up to a stranger and they would know the thing I never wanted to tell people. "My name is Jessica Harris, and I struggled with pornography." But I've learned that just because that's what you know doesn't mean that's who I am.

Years ago, I shared my story of pornography addiction on a blog I never wanted anyone to find. Well, people found it, and I've had the opportunity to travel the world sharing the message of God's grace. I've helped ministries create material and programs to minister to women hidden by shame. But I've learned that just because that's what I do doesn't mean that's who I am.

I'm Jessica, a wife, a mom, a friend, and a lover of good food, loose-leaf tea, and long walks in the woods. I am also a writer and a speaker, even though I didn't like English class and always get stage fright. I believe in loving people extravagantly and am forever thankful for grace. God loved me. God redeemed me. He calls me his own. His beloved.

And that's who I am.

Find more of my story, writing, and free resources, including study questions for this book, at beggarsdaughter.com.

JESSICA HARRIS provides awareness, support, and resources for Christian women struggling with an addiction to pornography. Visit her website, beggarsdaughter.com, to receive inspirational content and subscribe to her newsletter.

CONNECT WITH THE AUTHOR ON SOCIAL MEDIA:

Beggars.Daughter   BeggarsDaughter